SELEC[illegible] PRAYERS

مختارات من الدعاء

A Collection of Du‘ā’ from the Qur’ān and Sunnah

Compiled by
Dr. Jamal A. Badawi

Ta-Ha Publishers Ltd.
www.taha.co.uk

First Published in 1979
7th Revised Edition Published June 2006
Reprinted June 2009
Reprinted May 2015

Published by
Ta-Ha Publishers Ltd.
Unit 4, Windsor Centre,
London, SE27 9NT
www.taha.co.uk

Compiled by: Dr. Jamal A. Badawi
General Editor: Dr. Abia Afsar-Siddiqui

Typeset by:
Planman I:TES (India)
Pvt Ltd

ISBN-13: 978 1842 000 77 9
Printed and bound by: Mega Basim, Turkey

Table of Contents

PREFACE VI

INTRODUCTION VIII

TRANSLITERATION SYSTEM XI

CHAPTER ONE: DU‘Ā’ FROM THE QUR’ĀN 1

I. *On Īmān (Faith)* 2
- Confirmation of Īmān 2
- Glorification of Allāh 4
- Submission to and Dependence on Allāh 11

II. Supplication 16
- Seeking Guidance 16
- Seeking Forgiveness (*Istighfār*) 17
- Seeking Knowledge and Wisdom 20
- Prayer for Patience, Perseverance and Steadfastness 21
- Seeking Provisions 24

III. Seeking the Protection of Allāh 25

IV. Offering of Thanks 29

V. Prayers for Family 31

VI. General 35

CHAPTER TWO: DU‘Ā’ FROM SUNNAH: *AL-MA’THŪRĀT* 38

CHAPTER THREE: DAILY DU‘Ā’ 47
- Waking up 48
- When entering the bathroom 48
- When leaving the bathroom 48
- While making Wuḍū’ (ablution) 49
- After completing Wuḍū’ 49
- After Adhān is complete 50
- When leaving the house 50

When going to the Mâsjid (mosque) 51
When entering the Mâsjid 51
After completing Ṣalāh 52
When leaving the Mâsjid 52
When entering the house 53
When beginning the meal 53
When finishing the meal 54
While undressing 54
While getting dressed 54
When mounting a means of transportation
(car, train, plane etc.) 55
When retiring to sleep 55

CHAPTER FOUR: DU'Ā' FOR SPECIAL OCCASIONS.................. 57

I. In Personal Life 58
When looking in the mirror 58
In case of insomnia 58
After a pleasant dream 59
After an unpleasant dream 59
On waking up after a nightmare 60

II. On Social Occasions 61
When you see a Muslim brother smiling 61
When told 'I love you' 61
When a favour is done to you 61
To someone who has got married 62
At the beginning of intercourse 62
Prayer for small children 62
At the end of meetings or gatherings 63

III. On the Occasion of Travel 64
What to say to someone who is leaving 64
When bidding farwell (by the traveller) 65
When setting out on a journey 65
Upon returning from a journey 66

IV. In Distress 67
When faced by a hardship 67
When a hope or desire could not be fulfilled 67
When feeling angry 68
When overwhelmed by a problem 68

When in pain (while placing one's hand over the location of the pain) 68
W.hen visiting a sick person (while patting the sick person) 69
At a time of disaster 69
When offering condolences (to the family of the deceased) 70
When visiting the graveyard 70

V. Others 72
Prayer for fulfillment of a need (*Ṣalātul Ḥājah*) 72
When seeking guidance in decision-making (*Istikhārah*) 73
When one wakes up for night prayers (*Tâhâjjûd*) 75

PREFACE

My gratitude is due to Allāh ﷻ for being able to make this book on du‘ā’ available to our English-speaking brothers and sisters. The book contains both the transliteration and the translation of each du‘ā’, in addition to the Arabic. It is hoped that this dual feature will help in reciting the du‘ā’ and in understanding what is being recited.

I pray to Allāh that He blesses those who use these du‘ā’ in inculcating a relationship of nearness to Him and in responding to His eternal loving call.

وَإِذَا سَأَلَكَ عِبَادِي عَنِّي فَإِنِّي قَرِيبٌ ۖ أُجِيبُ دَعْوَةَ الدَّاعِ إِذَا دَعَانِ ۖ
فَلْيَسْتَجِيبُوا لِي وَلْيُؤْمِنُوا بِي لَعَلَّهُمْ يَرْشُدُونَ

When My servants ask thee concerning me, I am indeed close (to them): I listen to the prayer of every suppliant when he calleth on Me: Let them also, with a will, listen to My call and believe in Me that they may walk in the right way. (2:186)

The idea to compile a book of du‘ā’ developed in the summer of 1977, in the course of my participation in the Imam Training Programs. It was then that several brothers and sisters expressed the wish that the du‘ā’ which they were learning orally might well be published in a book to be made available to all those who wished to recite and benefit from them.

The first chapter of this book was compiled following a review of the Qur’ān and taking note of the āyāt or their portions which constitute du‘ā’. These were then studied and classified under their main subject headings. The remaining du‘ā’ in chapters 2, 3 and 4 were selected and compiled from Hasan al-Bânnā’s *Al-Mathūrāt*, an excellent collection of du‘ā’. The order of some du‘ā’ in Chapters 3 and 4 differ slightly from that in *Al-Ma’thūrāt*.

All transliteration has been done by the author according to the system indicated in the book. The translations of the Qur’ānic du‘ā’ have been taken from

Yūsuf Ali's The Glorious Qur'ān. The other du'ā' in Chapters 2, 3 and 4 have been translated by the author. The footnotes indicate the source of the du'ā' and in some cases a brief comment on it.

Brother Anwer Beg, Editor of Publications in the ITC, has been very helpful in editing this work and in other related matters.

Dr. Jamal A. Badawi

Introduction [1]

Meaning of *Dhikr*

Dhikr literally means remembrance. As used in this book, it refers to the remembrance of Allāh ﷾ [2]. The Qur'ān refers to itself as *dhikr*[3]. As the Word of Allāh ﷾, it helps us to remember Him in all our thoughts and deeds.

Dhikr at all times

Each human being pursues an ultimate and fundamental goal in life. This goal constitutes one's ideal, the focal point of one's thoughts, aspirations and activities. The loftier and nobler the goal is, the more sublime are the thoughts and deeds emanating from it. The basic message of Islam is to elevate the soul, to purify and uplift it to the highest possible plane. This cannot be accomplished unless Allāh ﷾ is our ultimate goal and the focus of our life. There is no wonder then that the Prophet ﷺ [4] used to engage in *dhikr* at all times.

Following the Prophet's example, *dhikr* should be made part of our daily life. *Dhikr* is not only limited to words; it also includes meditation, reflection, repentance, seeking lawful provisions and generally, every lawful act during which the presence of Allāh ﷾ is felt.

Rewards for *Dhikr*

Among the numerous passages in the Qur'ān which deal with *dhikr*, are the following:

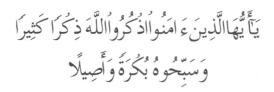

يَٰٓأَيُّهَا ٱلَّذِينَ ءَامَنُوا۟ ٱذْكُرُوا۟ ٱللَّهَ ذِكْرًا كَثِيرًا
وَسَبِّحُوهُ بُكْرَةً وَأَصِيلًا

[1] This introduction is based on Hasan al-Bânnā's *Al-Ma'thūrāt*, Maktabat-ul-Manār, Kuwait, nd, pp.5-12.

[2] This is the Arabic for *subhānahū wa ta'āla* meaning Glory be to Him, Most High.

[3] See 15:9

[4] This is the Arabic for *sallallāhu alayhi wa sallam* meaning peace and blessings of Allāh be upon him.

هُوَ الَّذِى يُصَلِّى عَلَيْكُمْ وَمَلَٰٓئِكَتُهُۥ لِيُخْرِجَكُم مِّنَ الظُّلُمَٰتِ إِلَى
النُّورِ ۚ وَكَانَ بِالْمُؤْمِنِينَ رَحِيمًا

O ye who believe! Celebrate the praises of Allāh and do this often; and glorify Him morning and evening. He it is Who sends blessings on you, as do His angels, that He may bring you out from the depths of darkness into light; And He is full of Mercy to the believers. (33:41-43)

إِنَّ الْمُسْلِمِينَ وَالْمُسْلِمَٰتِ وَالْمُؤْمِنِينَ وَالْمُؤْمِنَٰتِ وَالْقَٰنِتِينَ
وَالْقَٰنِتَٰتِ وَالصَّٰدِقِينَ وَالصَّٰدِقَٰتِ وَالصَّٰبِرِينَ وَالصَّٰبِرَٰتِ
وَالْخَٰشِعِينَ وَالْخَٰشِعَٰتِ وَالْمُتَصَدِّقِينَ وَالْمُتَصَدِّقَٰتِ وَالصَّٰٓئِمِينَ
وَالصَّٰٓئِمَٰتِ وَالْحَٰفِظِينَ فُرُوجَهُمْ وَالْحَٰفِظَٰتِ وَالذَّٰكِرِينَ اللَّهَ
كَثِيرًا وَالذَّٰكِرَٰتِ أَعَدَّ اللَّهُ لَهُم مَّغْفِرَةً وَأَجْرًا عَظِيمًا

For Muslim men and women, for believing men and women, for devout men and women, for true men and women, for men and women who are patient and constant, for men and women who humble themselves, for men and women who give in charity, for men and women who fast (and deny themselves), for men and women who guard their chastity and for men and women who engage much in Allāh's praise. For them Allāh has prepared forgiveness and great reward. (33:35)

In a ḥadīth Qudsi, the Prophet ﷺ reported that Allāh سبحانه وتعالى said, "I (will respond according to) what my servant thinks of Me, and I am with him when he remembers Me. So if he remembers Me in secret then I will remember him in secret and if he remembers Me in a group, I will remember him in a better group." (Al-Bukhāri and Muslim)

Manners in *Dhikr*

To be of benefit, the following points should be observed during *dhikr*:
a) Humility, sobriety and reflection on the meaning of the du‘ā’
b) Cleanliness and respectability with regards to clothing and place of *dhikr*
c) Lowering the voice and avoiding disruption to others engaged in *dhikr*

وَاذْكُر رَّبَّكَ فِي نَفْسِكَ تَضَرُّعًا وَخِيفَةً وَدُونَ الْجَهْرِ مِنَ
الْقَوْلِ بِالْغُدُوِّ وَالْآصَالِ وَلَا تَكُن مِّنَ الْغَافِلِينَ

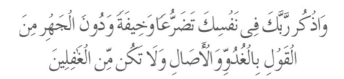

And do thou (O reader!) bring thy Lord to remembrance in thy (very) soul with humility and in reverence, without loudness in words, in the mornings and evenings; and be not thou of those who are unheedful. (7:205)

By observing these rules, the person will feel happiness in the heart, light in the soul and the blessing of Allāh ﷻ.

Dhikr in a group

Engaging in *dhikr* is permissible in groups. Indeed, according to some aḥadīth, it is encouraged:

The Prophet ﷺ said, “If a group of people sit together remembering Allāh (i.e. engaging in *dhikr*), the angels will circle them, the mercy will shroud them, the peace will descend onto them, and Allāh will remember them among those with Him.” (Muslim)

Indeed *dhikr* in a group may help teach those who do not know the desired du‘ā’ and bring Muslims’ hearts together and strengthen their noble ties.

Transliteration System

In transliterating Arabic words, the following system of symbols has been used.

I. Arabic consonants with English Equivalents

Arabic	English	Example	Arabic	English	Example
ب	b	book	ش	sh	shield
ت	t	toy	ف	f	fast
ث	th	three	ك	k	key
ج	j	joy	ل	l	light
د	d	door	م	m	mother
ذ	dh	this	ن	n	number
ر	r	ran	ه	h	humble
ز	z	zeal	و	w,ao	Laos
س	s	sand	ى	y	yard

II. Arabic consonants with no English equivalent

Arabic	English	Example	Arabic	English	Example
ء	’	Qur’ān	ط	ṭ	Ṭaharah
ح	ḥ	Ḥasan	ظ	ẓ	Ẓuhr
خ	kh	Khomaini	ع	‘	‘Abdullah
ص	ṣ	Ṣahih	غ	gh	Ghayb
ض	ḍ	Wuḍu	ق	q	Qur’ān

III. **Elongation:** A macron indicates long vowels:

ā should be long (aa) as in band or Qur'ān

ī should be long (ee) as in peel or ḥadīth

ū should be long (oo) as in tooth or Qunūt

IV. **Shortening:** A circumflex indicates shortened vowels:

â should be pronounced as in woman

î should be pronounced as in with

û should be pronounced as in Sûnnah

V. **Assimilation** of the definite article (*al*) in Arabic

When the above article (*al*) precedes a dental, sibilant n, t, r, the l is assimilated in pronunciation of the following letter. Therefore, in transliteration the word is written as it is pronounced not as it is actually written in Arabic. For example:

An-Nasā'i not Al-Nasā'i
At-Tirmidhi not Al-Tirmidhi
Ash-Shāfi'ī not Al- Shāfi'ī

Chapter One:

Du‘ā’ from the Qur’ān

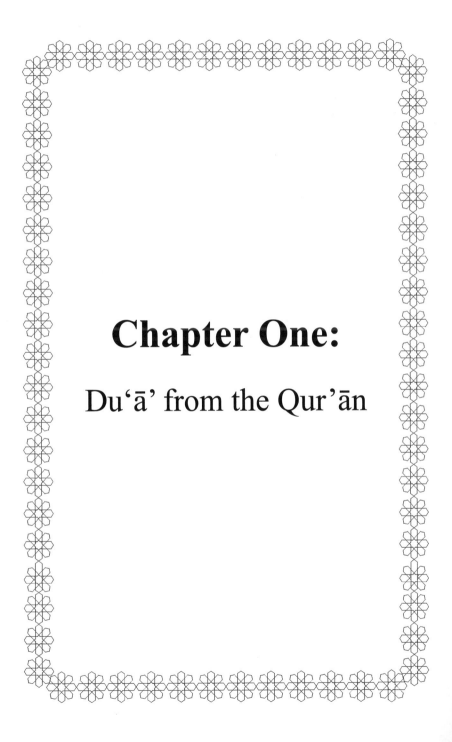

I. On Īmān (Faith)

Confirmation of Īmān

(1)

قُلْ إِنِّىٓ أُمِرْتُ أَنْ أَعْبُدَ ٱللَّهَ مُخْلِصًا لَّهُ ٱلدِّينَ
وَأُمِرْتُ لِأَنْ أَكُونَ أَوَّلَ ٱلْمُسْلِمِينَ

Qul innī ûmîrtû ân a'budâllāhâ mûkhlisâl lâhûddīn.
Wâ ûmîrtû li'ân akoonâ âwwâlâl muslimeen

Say: "Verily, I am commanded to serve Allāh with sincere devotion;
"And I am commanded to be the first of those who bow to
Allāh in Islām." (39:11-12)

(2)

رَبَّنَآ ءَامَنَّا بِمَآ أَنزَلْتَ وَٱتَّبَعْنَا ٱلرَّسُولَ
فَٱكْتُبْنَا مَعَ ٱلشَّٰهِدِينَ

Râbbânā āmannā bîmā ânzâltâ wâttâbâ'nârrâsoolâ
fâktûbnā mâ'âsh-shāhideen

"Our Lord! We believe in what Thou hast revealed and we follow the Apostle; then write us down among those who bear witness." (3:53)

---

(1) Sūrâh Az-Zumâr 39:11-12. Directed to the Prophet Muḥâmmâd ﷺ.

(2) Sūrâh Āli 'Imrān 3:53. Prayers of the disciples of Prophet 'Isa عليه السلام in response to his call for helpers.

(3)

رَبُّنَا رَبُّ السَّمَٰوَٰتِ وَالْأَرْضِ لَن نَّدْعُوَا
مِن دُونِهِۦٓ إِلَٰهًا ۖ لَّقَدْ قُلْنَآ إِذًا شَطَطًا

Râbbûnā râbbûs-sâmāwāti wâl’arḍi lân-nâd‘ûwâ
min doonihī ilāha. Lâqâd qûlnā idhân shâṭâṭā

“Our Lord is the Lord of the heavens and of the earth: never shall we call upon any god other than Him: if we did, we should indeed have uttered an enormity!” (18:14)

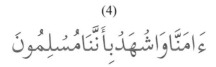

(4)

ءَامَنَّا وَاشْهَدْ بِأَنَّنَا مُسْلِمُونَ

Āmânnā wâsh-hâd bi’ânnânā muslimoon

“We have faith and do thou bear witness that we bow to Allāh as Muslims.” (5:111)

(5)

قُلْ أَتُحَآجُّونَنَا فِى اللَّهِ وَهُوَ رَبُّنَا وَرَبُّكُمْ وَلَنَآ
أَعْمَٰلُنَا وَلَكُمْ أَعْمَٰلُكُمْ وَنَحْنُ لَهُۥ مُخْلِصُونَ

Qul atuḥājjūnânā fil-lāhī wâhuwâ râbbûnā wârâbbûkûm wâlânā
a‘mālûna wâlâkûm a‘mālûkûm wâ nâḥnû lâhū mûkhlisoon

---

(3) Sūrâh Al-Kahf: 18:14. Prayer of the ‘People of the Cave’ in rejection to the polytheism practised by their people.

(4) Sūrâh Al-Mā’idah 5:111. Prayer of the disciples of Prophet ‘Isa عليه السلام. It shows that all those who bowed to Allāh’s will were ‘Muslims’.

(5) Sūrâh Al-Bâqârâh 2:139. In response to Jews and Christians who argued that by becoming Jew or Christian, one is guided to salvation. The preceding āyāt show that Ibrāhīm عليه السلام and his descendents were nothing but upright Muslims.

Say: Will ye dispute with us about Allāh, seeing that He is our Lord and your Lord; that we are responsible for our doings and ye for yours; and that we are sincere (in our faith) in Him? (2:139)

(6)

قُلْ هَٰذِهِۦ سَبِيلِىٓ أَدْعُوٓا۟ إِلَى ٱللَّهِ ۚ عَلَىٰ بَصِيرَةٍ
أَنَا۠ وَمَنِ ٱتَّبَعَنِى ۖ وَسُبْحَٰنَ ٱللَّهِ وَمَآ أَنَا۠ مِنَ ٱلْمُشْرِكِينَ

Qul hādhihi sâbeelī ad'oo ilâl-lāhi 'âlā baṣīrâtin
anā wâmânit-tâbâ'âni wâ subhānâllāhi wâmā anā minâl mushrikeen

Say thou: "This is my way: I do invite unto Allāh, - on evidence clear as the seeing with one's eyes, - I and whoever follows me. Glory to Allāh! And never will I join gods with Allāh!" (12:108)

Glorification of Allāh

(7)

سُبْحَٰنَ رَبِّ ٱلسَّمَٰوَٰتِ وَٱلْأَرْضِ رَبِّ ٱلْعَرْشِ عَمَّا يَصِفُونَ

Subḥānâ râbbis-sâmāwātī wâl'arḍī râbbil'arshî 'ammā yaṣifoon

Glory to the Lord of the heavens and the earth, the Lord of the Throne (of Authority)! (He is free) from the things they attribute (to Him)! (43:82)

---

(6) Sūrâh Yūsuf 12:108. Follows āyāt which point out to those who pass by countless signs of Allāh's presence and attributes, also to those whose nominal faith in Allāh ﷻ does not shield them from associating other gods with Allāh ﷻ and deifying mortals.

(7) Sūrâh Az-Zukhrûf 43:82. Directed to Prophet Muḥâmmâd ﷺ. It glorifies Allāh ﷻ from attributing a son to Him.

(8)

سُبۡحَٰنَ ٱللَّهِ عَمَّا يُشۡرِكُونَ

Subḥānâl-lāhi 'ammā yûshrikoon

Glory to Allāh! (High is He) above the partners they attribute to Him. (59:23)

(9)

تَبَٰرَكَ ٱسۡمُ رَبِّكَ ذِى ٱلۡجَلَٰلِ وَٱلۡإِكۡرَامِ

Tâbārâkâsmû râbbikâ dhil jâlālî wâl-ikrām

Blessed be the name of thy Lord, full of Majesty, Bounty and Honour. (55:78)

(10)

سُبۡحَٰنَهُۥ وَتَعَٰلَىٰ عَمَّا يَصِفُونَ

بَدِيعُ ٱلسَّمَٰوَٰتِ وَٱلۡأَرۡضِۖ أَنَّىٰ يَكُونُ لَهُۥ وَلَدٌ وَلَمۡ تَكُن لَّهُۥ

صَٰحِبَةٌۖ وَخَلَقَ كُلَّ شَىۡءٍۖ وَهُوَ بِكُلِّ شَىۡءٍ عَلِيمٌ

Subḥānâhū wât'ālā 'ammā yaṣifoon.
Bâdī'us-sâmāwātî wâl'arḍ. Annā yâkoonû lâhū wâlâdun wâlâm tâkun lâhū ṣāhîbatuw-wâkhâlâqâ kullâ shây'. Wâhuwâ bikullî shây'in 'âleem

Praise and glory be to Him! (For He is) above what they attribute to Him! To Him is due the primal origin of the heavens and the earth: How can He have a son when He hath no consort? He created all things, and He hath full knowledge of all things. (6:100-101)

---

(8) Sūrâh Al-Hashr 59:23. This is part of 3 āyāt containing 14 of the attributes of Allāh (59:22-24).

(9) Sūrâh Ar-Râhmān 55:78. Concludes Sūrâh Ar-Râhmān whose basic theme is the Bounty and Majesty of Allāh ﷻ and man's duty to acknowledge them.

(10) Sūrâh Al-Anām 6:100-101. In response to those who made the Jinn equals with Allāh ﷻ and attributed to Him sons and daughters.

(11)

إِنَّمَا اللَّهُ إِلَٰهٌ وَاحِدٌ ۖ سُبْحَٰنَهُۥٓ أَن يَكُونَ لَهُۥ وَلَدٌ ۘ لَّهُۥ مَا فِى
السَّمَٰوَٰتِ وَمَا فِى الْأَرْضِ ۗ وَكَفَىٰ بِاللَّهِ وَكِيلًا

Innâmâllāhu ilāhuw-wāḥid. Subḥānâhu ay-yâkoonâ lâhū wâlâd. Lâhū mā fis-sâmāwātî wâmâ fil-arḍ. Wâ kâfā billāhi wâkeelā

For Allāh is One God: Glory be to Him: (Far Exalted is He) above having a son. To Him belong all things in the heavens and on earth. And enough is Allāh as a disposer of affairs. (4:171)

(12)

فَتَبَارَكَ اللَّهُ أَحْسَنُ الْخَٰلِقِينَ

Fâ tâbārâkâl-lāhû aḥsânul khāliqeen

So blessed be Allāh, the Best to create! (23:14)

(13)

وَتَبَارَكَ الَّذِى لَهُۥ مُلْكُ السَّمَٰوَٰتِ وَالْأَرْضِ
وَمَا بَيْنَهُمَا وَعِندَهُۥ عِلْمُ السَّاعَةِ وَإِلَيْهِ تُرْجَعُونَ

Wâ tâbārâkâl-lâdhī lâhū mûlkûs-sâmāwāti wâl'arḍi
wâmā bâynâhumā wâ 'indâhū 'ilmus-sā'âti wâ'ilayhi tûrjâ'oon

And Blessed is He to Whom belongs the dominion of the heavens and the earth, and all between them: With Him is the knowledge of the Hour (of Judgement): And to Him shall ye be brought back. (43:85)

---

(11) Sūrâh An-Nisā' 4:171. In rejection of the trinity.

(12) Sūrâh Al-Mu'minūn 23:14. Concludes 3 āyāt which give an amazing description of the foetal stages.

(13) Sūrâh Az-Zukhrûf 43:85

(14)

تَبَارَكَ الَّذِى جَعَلَ فِى السَّمَآءِ بُرُوجًا وَجَعَلَ فِيهَا سِرَاجًا وَقَمَرًا مُّنِيرًا

Tâbārâkâl-lâdhī jâ'âlâ fis-sâmā'î bûroojaw wâjâ'âlâ fihā sirājâw wâ qâmârâm muneerā

Blessed is He Who made constellations in the skies, and placed therein a lamp and a moon giving light. (25:61)

(15)

أَلَا لَهُ الْخَلْقُ وَالْأَمْرُ تَبَارَكَ اللَّهُ رَبُّ الْعَلَمِينَ

Alā lâhûl-khâlqû wâl'amrû tâbārâkâl-lāhû râbbul'ālâmīn

And to govern? Blessed be Allāh, the Cherisher and Sustainer of the Worlds! (7:54)

(16)

فَسَبِّحْ بِاسْمِ رَبِّكَ الْعَظِيمِ

Fâ sâbbiḥ bismî râbbikâl 'âẓeem.

So celebrate with praises the name of thy Lord the Supreme. (56:96)

---

(14) Sūrâh Al-Furqān 25:61

(15) Sūrâh Al-A'rāf 7:54. Shows that the establishment of an Islamic government is an acknowledgement of Allāh's ﷻ right to govern, being the Creator.

(16) Sūrâh Al-Wāqi'ah 56:96

(17)

فَسَبِّحْ بِحَمْدِ رَبِّكَ وَكُن مِّنَ السَّٰجِدِينَ

Fâ sâbbiḥ biḥâmdî râbbikâ wâkum-minâs sājideen

But celebrate the praises of thy Lord and be of those who prostrate themselves in adoration. (15:98)

(18)

سُبْحَٰنَ رَبِّنَآ إِن كَانَ وَعْدُ رَبِّنَا لَمَفْعُولًا

Subḥānâ râbbinā in kānâ wâ'dû râbbinā lâmâf'oolā

"Glory to our Lord! Truly has the promise of our Lord been fulfilled!" (17:108)

(19)

فَسُبْحَٰنَ اللَّهِ حِينَ تُمْسُونَ وَحِينَ تُصْبِحُونَ

Fâ subḥānâl-lāhî ḥeenâ tûmsoonâ wâ ḥeenâ tûṣbiḥoon

So (give) glory to Allāh when ye reach eventide and when ye rise in the morning. (30:17)

---

(17) Sūrâh Al-Hijr 15:98. Instructions to Prophet Muḥâmmâd ﷺ when he was distressed at what the unbelievers said.

(18) Sūrâh Al-Isrā' 17:108. Describes the reaction of the sincere among those who received previous revelations upon hearing the Qur'ān. They saw in the Qur'ān and in Muḥâmmâd ﷺ the fulfilment of Allāh's ﷻ promise in previous scriptures.

(19) Sūrâh Ar-Rūm 30:17

(20)

رَبَّنَا مَا خَلَقْتَ هَٰذَا بَٰطِلًا سُبْحَٰنَكَ فَقِنَا عَذَابَ ٱلنَّارِ

Râbbânā mā-khâlâqtâ hādhā bạtilân subḥānâkâ fâqinā 'adhāban-nār

"Our Lord! Not for naught hast Thou created (all) this! Glory to Thee! Give us salvation from the penalty of the Fire." (3:191)

(21)

فَسُبْحَٰنَ ٱلَّذِى بِيَدِهِۦ مَلَكُوتُ كُلِّ شَىْءٍ وَإِلَيْهِ تُرْجَعُونَ

Fâ subḥānâl-lâdhī bîyâdihī mâlâkootû kullî shây'iw wâ'ilayhî tûrjâ'oon

So glory to Him in Whose hands is the dominion of all things: And to Him will ye be all brought back. (36:83)

(22)

تَبَٰرَكَ ٱلَّذِى بِيَدِهِ ٱلْمُلْكُ وَهُوَ عَلَىٰ كُلِّ شَىْءٍ قَدِيرٌ

Tâbārâkâl-lâdhī biyâdîhîl mulkû wâhuwâ 'alā kullî shây'in qâdeer

Blessed be He in whose hands is Dominion; And He over all things hath Power. (67:1)

(23)

ذَٰلِكُمُ ٱللَّهُ رَبُّكُمْ فَتَبَارَكَ ٱللَّهُ رَبُّ ٱلْعَٰلَمِينَ

Dhālikumul-lāhû râbbûkum fâtâbārâkâllāhû râbbûl 'ālâmeen

---

(20) Sūrâh Āli-'Imrān 3:191. Believers' reaction when they contemplate the wonders of creation in the heavens and earth.

(21) Sūrâh Yā-Sīn 36:83. Conclusion of Sūrâh Yā-Sīn. As everything was created and maintained by Allāh ﷻ so everything will go back to Him.

(22) Sūrâh Al-Mûlk 67:1

(23) Sūrâh Ghāfir 40:64

Such is Allāh your Lord. So Glory to Allāh, the Lord of the Worlds! (40:64)

(24)

سَبِّحِ اسْمَ رَبِّكَ الْأَعْلَى

Sâbbîḥîsmâ râbbikâl a'lā

Glorify the name of thy Guardian-Lord Most High. (87:1)

(25)

فَسَبِّحْ بِحَمْدِ رَبِّكَ وَاسْتَغْفِرْهُ إِنَّهُۥ كَانَ تَوَّابًا

Fâ sâbbiḥ biḥâmdî râbbikâ wâstâghfirh. Innâhū kānâ tâwwābā

Celebrate the praises of thy Lord and pray for His forgiveness: For He is Oft-Returning (in Grace and Mercy). (110:3)

(26)

يُسَبِّحُ لِلَّهِ مَا فِي السَّمَوَٰتِ وَمَا فِي الْأَرْضِ لَهُ الْمُلْكُ
وَلَهُ الْحَمْدُ وَهُوَ عَلَىٰ كُلِّ شَيْءٍ قَدِيرٌ

Yusâbbiḥû lillāhî māfis-sâmāwātî wâmā fil arḍ. Lâhul mulkû wâlâhul ḥamd. Wâhuwâ 'alā kullî shây'in qâdeer

Whatever is in the heavens and on earth doth declare the praises and glory of Allāh: to Him belongs Dominion and to Him belongs praise and He has power over all things. (64:1)

---

(24) Sūrâh Al-A'lā 87:1

(25) Sūrâh An-Nasr 110:3. At the glorious moment of the Prophet's return to Mâkkâh and when people were embracing Islām in crowds, the Prophet ﷺ is reminded to humbly praise Allāh for the victory He gave to the believers.

(26) Sūrâh At-Taghābun 64:1

Submission to and Dependence on Allāh

(27)

وَلِلَّهِ غَيْبُ ٱلسَّمَٰوَٰتِ وَٱلْأَرْضِ وَإِلَيْهِ يُرْجَعُ ٱلْأَمْرُ كُلُّهُۥ فَٱعْبُدْهُ وَتَوَكَّلْ عَلَيْهِ ۚ وَمَا رَبُّكَ بِغَٰفِلٍ عَمَّا تَعْمَلُونَ

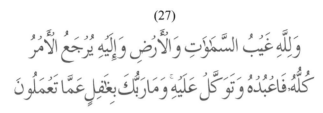

Wâlillāhi ghâybus-sâmāwātî wâl'arḍ. Wâ'ilayhî yurjâ'ul amrû kûlluh. Fâ'bûdhû wâtâwâkkâl 'alâyh wâmā râbbukâ bighāfilin 'ammā tâ'mâloon

To Allāh do belong the unseen (secrets) of the heavens and the earth and to Him goeth back every affair (for decision): Then worship Him and put thy trust in Him and thy Lord is not unmindful of aught that ye do. (11:123)

(28)

إِنِّى تَوَكَّلْتُ عَلَى ٱللَّهِ رَبِّى وَرَبِّكُم ۚ مَّا مِن دَآبَّةٍ إِلَّا هُوَ ءَاخِذٌۢ بِنَاصِيَتِهَآ ۚ إِنَّ رَبِّى عَلَىٰ صِرَٰطٍ مُّسْتَقِيمٍ

Innī tâwâkkâltû 'alâl-lāhi râbbī wârâbbīkum mā min dābbâtin illā hûwâ ākhidhum bînāṣiyâtihā. Innâ râbbī 'alā ṣirātim mustâqeem

"I put my trust in Allāh, my Lord and your Lord! There is not a moving creature but He hath grasp of its forelock. Verily, it is my Lord that is on a straight path." (11:56)

(29)

أَسْلَمْتُ وَجْهِىَ لِلَّهِ وَمَنِ ٱتَّبَعَنِ

Aslâmtû wâjhiyâ lillāhî wâmânit-tabâ'ân

---

(27) Sūrâh Hūd 11:123

(28) Sūrâh Hūd 11:56. Prayer of Prophet Hūd عليه السلام.

(29) Sūrâh Āli-'Imrān 3:20

"I have submitted my whole self to Allāh and so have those who follow me." (3:20)

(30)

قُلْ هُوَ الرَّحْمَٰنُ ءَامَنَّا بِهِۦ وَعَلَيْهِ تَوَكَّلْنَا ۖ فَسَتَعْلَمُونَ
مَنْ هُوَ فِى ضَلَٰلٍ مُّبِينٍ

Qul huwâr-râḥmānû āmânnā bihī wâ'alayhî tâwâkkâlnā. Fâsâtâ'lâmoonâ mân huwâ fi ḍâlālim-mûbeen

Say: "He is (Allāh) Most Gracious: we have believed in Him and on Him have we put our trust. So soon will ye know which (of us) it is that is in manifest error." (67:29)

(31)

إِنَّ وَلِـِّۧىَ ٱللَّهُ ٱلَّذِى نَزَّلَ ٱلْكِتَٰبَ ۖ وَهُوَ يَتَوَلَّى ٱلصَّٰلِحِينَ

Innâ wâlīyyiyâl-lāhûl-lâdhī nâzzâlâl kitābâ wâhuwâ yâtâwâllâṣ-ṣaliḥeen

"For my protector is Allāh Who revealed the Book (from time to time) and He will choose and befriend the righteous." (7:196)

(32)

إِنِّى وَجَّهْتُ وَجْهِىَ لِلَّذِى فَطَرَ ٱلسَّمَٰوَٰتِ
وَٱلْأَرْضَ حَنِيفًا ۖ وَمَآ أَنَا۠ مِنَ ٱلْمُشْرِكِينَ

Innī wâjjâhtû wâjhiyâ lillâdhī fâṭârâs-sâmāwātî wâl'arḍâ ḥâneefaw-wâmā anā minâl mûshrikeen

---

(30) Sūrâh Al-Mulk 67:29

(31) Sūrâh Al-A'rāf 7:196

(32) Sūrâh Al-Anām 6:79. Prayer of Prophet Ibrāhīm عليه السلام.

"For me I have set my face, firmly and truly, towards Him Who created the heavens and the earth and never shall I give partners to Allāh." (6:79)

(33)

قُلْ إِنَّ صَلَاتِى وَنُسُكِى وَمَحْيَاىَ وَمَمَاتِى لِلَّهِ رَبِّ ٱلْعَٰلَمِينَ
لَا شَرِيكَ لَهُۥ ۖ وَبِذَٰلِكَ أُمِرْتُ وَأَنَا۠ أَوَّلُ ٱلْمُسْلِمِينَ

Qul innâ ṣâlātī wânûsûkī wâmâḥyāyâ wâmâmātī lîllāhî râbbîl 'ālâmeen la shâreekâ lâhū wâbidhālikâ ûmîrtû wâ'ânā âwwalûl muslimeen

Say: "Truly, my prayer and my service of sacrifice, my life and my death are (all) for Allāh, the Cherisher of the Worlds: No partner hath He: this I am commanded, and I am the first of those who bow to His will." (6:162-163)

(34)

رَبَّنَآ إِنَّكَ تَعْلَمُ مَا نُخْفِى وَمَا نُعْلِنُ ۗ وَمَا يَخْفَىٰ عَلَى ٱللَّهِ
مِن شَىْءٍ فِى ٱلْأَرْضِ وَلَا فِى ٱلسَّمَآءِ

Râbbânā innâkâ ta'lâmû mā nûkhfī wâmā nû'līnû wâmā yâkhfā 'alâllāhi min shây'in fil'ârḍi wâlā fis-sâmā'

"O our Lord! Truly Thou dost know what we conceal and what we reveal: For nothing whatever is hidden from Allāh whether on earth or in heaven." (14:38)

---

(33) Sūrâh Al-Anām 6:162-163

(34) Sūrâh Ibrāhīm 14:38. Prayer of Prophet Ibrāhīm عليه السلام.

(35)

قُلِ اللَّهُمَّ فَاطِرَ السَّمَٰوَٰتِ وَالْأَرْضِ عَٰلِمَ الْغَيْبِ وَالشَّهَٰدَةِ
أَنتَ تَحْكُمُ بَيْنَ عِبَادِكَ فِي مَا كَانُوا فِيهِ يَخْتَلِفُونَ

Qul-lil-lāhummâ fāṭirâs-sâmāwātî wâl'arḍî 'ālimâl ghâybî wâsh-shâhādâtî antâ tâḥkûmû bâynâ 'ibādikâ fīmā kānoo fīhî yâkhtâlifoon

Say: "O Allāh! Creator of the heavens and the earth! Knower of all that is hidden and open: It is Thou that wilt judge between Thy servants in those matters about which they have differed." (39:46)

(36)

الَّذِي خَلَقَنِي فَهُوَ يَهْدِينِ
وَالَّذِي هُوَ يُطْعِمُنِي وَيَسْقِينِ
وَإِذَا مَرِضْتُ فَهُوَ يَشْفِينِ
وَالَّذِي يُمِيتُنِي ثُمَّ يُحْيِينِ
وَالَّذِي أَطْمَعُ أَن يَغْفِرَ لِي خَطِيئَتِي يَوْمَ الدِّينِ

Allâdhī khâlâqânī fâhuwâ yâhdeen.
Wâllâdhī huwâ yuṭ'imunī wâyâsqeen.
Wa'idhā mâriḍtû fâhuwâ yâshfeen.
Wâllâdhī yumeetûnī thummâ yûḥyeen.
Wâllâdhī aṭmâ'û ay-yâghfirâ-lī khâṭee'âtī yawmâd-dīn.

"Who created me and it is He Who guides me; Who gives me food and drink; And when I am ill, it is He who cures me; Who will cause me to die and then to live (again); And Who, I hope, will forgive me my faults on the Day of Judgment." (26:78-82)

---

(35) Sūrâh Az-Zumâr 39:46

(36) Sūrâh Ash-Shu'arā 26:78-82

(37)

وَتَوَكَّلْ عَلَى الْحَيِّ الَّذِي لَا يَمُوتُ وَسَبِّحْ
بِحَمْدِهِۦ وَكَفَىٰ بِهِۦ بِذُنُوبِ عِبَادِهِۦ خَبِيرًا

Wâtâwâkkâl 'alâl ḥayyil lâdhī lā yâmootû wâsâbbiḥ bîḥâmdîh. Wâkâfā bihī bidhunoobî 'ibādihī khâbeerā

And put thy trust in Him Who lives and dies not; and celebrate His praise; and enough is He to be acquainted with the faults of His servants. (25:58)

---

(37) Sūrâh Al-Furqān 25:58

II. Supplication

Seeking Guidance

(38)

لَئِن لَّمْ يَهْدِنِى رَبِّى لَأَكُونَنَّ مِنَ الْقَوْمِ الضَّآلِّينَ

La'illâm yâhdînī râbbī lâ'akoonânnâ minâl qâwmiḍ-ḍālleen

"Unless my Lord guide me, I shall surely be among those who go astray." (6:77)

(39)

عَسَىٰ رَبِّىٓ أَن يَهْدِيَنِى سَوَآءَ السَّبِيلِ

'Asā râbbī ay-yâhdiyânī sâwā'âs-sâbeel

"I do hope that my Lord will show me the smooth and straight path." (28:22)

(40)

رَبَّنَآ ءَاتِنَا مِن لَّدُنكَ رَحْمَةً وَهَيِّئْ لَنَا مِنْ أَمْرِنَا رَشَدًا

Râbbânā ātînā mil-lâdûnka râḥmâtâw-wâhayyi' lânā min âmrinā râshâdā

"Our Lord! Bestow on us mercy from Thyself, and dispose of our affair for us in the right way." (18:10)

---

(38) Sūrâh Al-Anām 6:77. Prayer of Prophet Ibrāhīm عليه السلام in his search for truth and certitude.

(39) Sūrâh Al-Qaṣaṣ 28:22. Prayer of Prophet Mūsa عليه السلام when he left Egypt in a state of fear turning towards the land of Mâdyân.

(40) Sūrâh Al-Kahf 18:10. Prayer of the 'People of the Cave' when they went to the Cave.

(41)

رَبَّنَا لَا تُزِغْ قُلُوبَنَا بَعْدَ إِذْ هَدَيْتَنَا وَهَبْ لَنَا مِن لَّدُنكَ
رَحْمَةً إِنَّكَ أَنتَ الْوَهَّابُ

Râbbânā lā tûzigh quloobânā ba'dâ idh hâdâytânā wâhâb lânā mil-lâdunkâ râḥmâh. Innâkâ ântâl wâhhāb

"Our Lord!" (they say), "Let not our hearts deviate now after Thou hast guided us, but grant us mercy from Thine own Presence; for Thou are the Grantor of bounties without measure." (3:8)

Seeking Forgiveness (*Istighfār*)

(42)

لَّآ إِلَٰهَ إِلَّآ أَنتَ سُبْحَٰنَكَ إِنِّى كُنتُ مِنَ الظَّٰلِمِينَ

Lā-ilāhâ illā antâ subḥānâkâ innī kuntû minâẓ-ẓālimeen

"There is no god but Thou: Glory to Thee, I was indeed wrong!" (21:87)

(43)

رَبِّ إِنِّى ظَلَمْتُ نَفْسِى فَاغْفِرْ لِى

Râbbî innī ẓâlâmtû nâfsī faghfirlī

---

(41) Sūrâh Āli-'Imrān 3:8. It comes after warning in the previous āyâh of those 'in whose hearts is perversity' who follow the allegorical portions of the Qur'ān, 'seeking discord and searching for its hidden meanings' which are known only to Allāh ﷻ. It should be noted that in the above āyâh (3:7), there is a mandatory pause (*wâqf lāzîm*) after the word Allāh. This means that the hidden meanings of the allegorical portions of the Qur'ān are known exclusively to Allāh ﷻ and not shared even by those who are firmly grounded in knowledge.

(42) Sūrâh Al-Anbiyā' 21:87. This was the cry of Prophet Yūnus عليه السلام when he was swallowed by a whale.

(43) Sūrâh Al-Qaṣaṣ 28:16

"O my Lord! I have indeed wronged my soul! Do Thou then forgive me?" (28:16)

(44)

رَبَّنَآ إِنَّنَآ ءَامَنَّا فَاغْفِرْ لَنَا ذُنُوبَنَا وَقِنَا عَذَابَ النَّارِ

Râbbânā innânā āmânnā fâghfir-lânā dhunoobânā wâqînā 'adhābân-nār

"Our Lord! We have indeed believed: forgive us, then, our sins and save us from the agony of the Fire." (3:16)

(45)

سُبْحَٰنَ رَبِّنَآ إِنَّا كُنَّا ظَٰلِمِينَ

Subḥānâ râbbinā innā kunnā ẓālimeen

"Glory to our Lord! Verily we have been doing wrong!" (68:29)

(46)

رَبَّنَا لَا تُؤَاخِذْنَآ إِن نَّسِينَآ أَوْ أَخْطَأْنَا ۚ رَبَّنَا وَلَا تَحْمِلْ
عَلَيْنَآ إِصْرًا كَمَا حَمَلْتَهُۥ عَلَى الَّذِينَ مِن قَبْلِنَا ۚ رَبَّنَا
وَلَا تُحَمِّلْنَا مَا لَا طَاقَةَ لَنَا بِهِۦ ۖ وَاعْفُ عَنَّا وَاغْفِرْ لَنَا وَارْحَمْنَآ ۚ
أَنتَ مَوْلَىٰنَا فَانصُرْنَا عَلَى الْقَوْمِ الْكَٰفِرِينَ

---

(44) Sūrâh Āli-'Imrān 3:16

(45) Sūrâh Al-Qalam 68:29. This was the cry of the rich 'People of the Garden' who resolved to gather the fruits of the garden early in the morning before any indigent person came to request a share of the fruits. Overnight Allāh destroyed their garden. Next morning, they were shocked to see their garden like a desolate spot, at which time they realised the cause of their loss – greed.

(46) Sūrâh Al-Bâqârâh 2:286. This āyâh along with 2:284-285 are highly recommended for recitation at the beginning of the day and in the evening. (At-Tabârani and Al-Hakim)

Râbbânā lā tu'ākhidhnā in-nasīnā au akhta'nā. Râbbânā wâlā taḥmil 'alâynā iṣrân kâmā ḥâmâltâhū 'alâl lâdhīnâ min qâblinā. Râbbânā wâlā tuḥâmmilnā malā ṭāqâtâlânā bîh. Wa'fû 'annā wâghfirlânā wârḥâmnā antâ maulānā fânṣûrnā 'âlâl qawmil kāfireen

"Our Lord! Condemn us not if we forget or fall into error; Our Lord! Lay not upon us a burden like that which Thou didst lay on those before us; Our Lord! Lay not on us a burden greater than we have strength to bear. Blot out our sins and grant us forgiveness. Have mercy on us. Thou art our Protector. Help us against those who stand against faith." (2:286)

(47)

رَبَّنَا اغْفِرْ لَنَا وَلِإِخْوَٰنِنَا الَّذِينَ سَبَقُونَا بِالْإِيمَٰنِ وَلَا تَجْعَلْ
فِي قُلُوبِنَا غِلًّا لِّلَّذِينَ ءَامَنُوا رَبَّنَا إِنَّكَ رَءُوفٌ رَّحِيمٌ

Râbbânâghfir lânā wâl ikhwāninâl lâdhīnâ sâbâqoonā bil'īmānî wâlā tâj'âl fī qûloobinā ghillâl-lillâdhīnâ āmânoo. Râbbânā innâkâ râ'oofûr-râḥeem

"Our Lord! Forgive us and our brethren who came before us into the faith and leave not in our hearts rancour (or sense of injury) against those who have believed. Our Lord! Thou art indeed full of kindness, Most Merciful." (59:10)

(48)

وَقُل رَّبِّ اغْفِرْ وَارْحَمْ وَأَنتَ خَيْرُ الرَّٰحِمِينَ

Wâqur-râbbighfir wârḥâm wâ'antâ khayrûr-rāḥimeen

So say, "O my Lord! Grant Thou forgiveness and mercy, for Thou art the best of those who show mercy!" (23:118)

---

(47) Sūrâh Al-Ḥashr 59:10

(48) Sūrâh Al-Mu'minūn 23:118

(49)

سُبۡحَٰنَكَ تُبۡتُ إِلَيۡكَ وَأَنَا۠ أَوَّلُ ٱلۡمُؤۡمِنِينَ

Subḥānâkâ tûbtû 'ilâykâ wâ'ânā awwâlul mu'mineen

"Glory be to Thee! To Thee I turn in repentance and I am the first to believe." (7:143)

(50)

سَمِعۡنَا وَأَطَعۡنَاۖ غُفۡرَانَكَ رَبَّنَا وَإِلَيۡكَ ٱلۡمَصِيرُ

Sâmi'nā wa'aṭa'nā ghufrānâkâ râbbânā wâ'ilâykâl mâṣeer

"We hear and we obey; (we seek) Thy forgiveness, Our Lord, and to Thee is the end of all journeys." (2:285)

Seeking Knowledge and Wisdom

(51)

وَقُل رَّبِّ زِدۡنِي عِلۡمٗا

Wâqur-râbbî zidnī 'ilmā

"O my Lord! Advance me in knowledge." (20:114)

---

(49) Sūrâh Al-A'râf 7:143. Prayer of Prophet Mūsa عليه السلام upon recovering from a swoon in which he fell after asking Allāh ﷻ to let him (Mūsa) look at Him.

(50) Sūrâh Al-Bâqârâh 2:285

(51) Sūrâh Tā-Hā 20:114

(52)

رَبِّ هَبْ لِي حُكْمًا وَأَلْحِقْنِي بِالصَّٰلِحِينَ

Râbbî hâblī ḥukmaw-wâ'alḥiqnī biṣṣāliḥeen

"O my Lord! Bestow wisdom on me and join me with the righteous." (26:83)

Prayer for Patience, Perseverance and Steadfastness

(53)

رَبَّنَا اكْشِفْ عَنَّا الْعَذَابَ إِنَّا مُؤْمِنُونَ

Râbbânâk shif 'annâl 'adhābâ innā mu'minoon

"Our Lord! Remove the penalty from us, for we do really believe!" (44:12)

(54)

إِنَّمَا أَشْكُوا بَثِّي وَحُزْنِي إِلَى اللَّهِ

Innâmā ashkoo bâth-thi wâḥuznī 'illâllāh

"I only complain of my distraction and anguish to Allāh." (12:86)

---

(52) Sūrâh Ash-Shu'arā 26:83. Prayer of Prophet Ibrāhīm عليه السلام.

(53) Sūrâh Ad-Dukhān 44:12. Reference to people's cry during a (prophesised) famine which actually befell the Mâkkâns. May also refer to the Day of Resurrection.

(54) Sūrâh Yūsuf 12:86. Response of Prophet Ya'qoob عليه السلام when he was criticised by his children for endangering his health by continuing to remember his absent son, Yūsuf عليه السلام.

(55)

رَبَّنَآ أَفۡرِغۡ عَلَيۡنَا صَبۡرٗا وَثَبِّتۡ أَقۡدَامَنَا
وَٱنصُرۡنَا عَلَى ٱلۡقَوۡمِ ٱلۡكَٰفِرِينَ

Râbbânā âfrigh 'alâynā ṣâbraw-wâthâbbit aqdāmânā
wânṣurnā 'alâl qawmil kāfireen

"Our Lord! Pour out constancy on us and make our steps firm: Help us against those that reject faith." (2:250)

(56)

رَبَّنَآ أَفۡرِغۡ عَلَيۡنَا صَبۡرٗا وَتَوَفَّنَا مُسۡلِمِينَ

Râbbânā âfrigh 'alâynā ṣâbraw-wâtâwâffânā muslimeen

"Our Lord! Pour out on us patience and constancy and take our souls unto Thee as Muslims (who bow to Thy will)!" (7:126)

(57)

وَٱصۡبِرۡ وَمَا صَبۡرُكَ إِلَّا بِٱللَّهِۚ وَلَا تَحۡزَنۡ عَلَيۡهِمۡ
وَلَا تَكُ فِي ضَيۡقٖ مِّمَّا يَمۡكُرُونَ
إِنَّ ٱللَّهَ مَعَ ٱلَّذِينَ ٱتَّقَواْ وَّٱلَّذِينَ هُم مُّحۡسِنُونَ

Wâṣbir wâmā ṣâbrûkâ illā billāh. Wâlā taḥzân 'alâyhim
wâla tâkû fī ḍâyqim mimmā yâmkûroon.
Innâllāhâ mâ'âl lâdhīnât-tâqau wâllâdhīnâ hum-muḥsinoon

---

(55) Sūrâh Al-Bâqârâh 2:250. The prayer of the remaining Israelites who stayed with their commander, Talūt, when they advanced to meet Jalūt and his forces.

(56) Sūrâh Al-A'rāf 7:126. Prayer of the Egyptian sorcerers (magicians) who believed in Prophet Mūsa عليه السلام when their pharaoh threatened them with mutilation and crucifixion.

(57) Sūrâh An-Naḥl 16:127-128

And do thou be patient, for thy patience is but from Allāh; nor grieve over them: and distress not thyself because of their plots, for Allāh is with those who restrain themselves and those who do good. (16:127-128)

(58)

قُلْ كَفَىٰ بِاللَّهِ شَهِيدًا بَيْنِى وَبَيْنَكُمْ إِنَّهُۥ كَانَ بِعِبَادِهِۦ خَبِيرًا بَصِيرًا

Qul kâfā billāhi shâheedâm bâynī wâ bâynâkum innâhū kānâ bi'ibādihī khâbeerâm bâṣeera

Say: "Enough is Allāh for a witness between me and you: for He is well acquainted with His servants and He sees (all things)." (17:96)

(59)

وَمَا لَنَآ أَلَّا نَتَوَكَّلَ عَلَى اللَّهِ وَقَدْ هَدَىٰنَا سُبُلَنَا وَلَنَصْبِرَنَّ عَلَىٰ مَآ ءَاذَيْتُمُونَا وَعَلَى اللَّهِ فَلْيَتَوَكَّلِ الْمُتَوَكِّلُونَ

Wâmā lânā allā nâtâwâkkâlâ 'alâl-lāhi wâqâd hâdānā sûbûlânā wâlânâṣbirânnâ 'alā mā ādhaytumoonā wâ 'âlâl-lāhi fâlyâtâwâkkâlil mutâwâkkiloon

"No reason have we why we should not put our trust on Allāh. Indeed He has guided us to the Ways we (follow). We shall certainly bear with patience all the hurt you may cause us. For those who put their trust should put their trust on Allāh." (14:12)

---

(58) Sūrâh Al-Isrā' 17:96

(59) Sūrâh Ibrāhīm 14:12. Prayer of the apostles in the face of their peoples' rejection of the truth.

Seeking Provisions

(60)

رَبِّ إِنِّى لِمَآ أَنزَلْتَ إِلَىَّ مِنْ خَيْرٍ فَقِيرٌ

Râbbî innī lîmā ânzâltâ ilâyyâ min khâyrin fâqeer

"O my Lord! Truly am I in (desperate) need of any good that Thou dost send me!" (28:24)

(61)

رَبِّ اشْرَحْ لِى صَدْرِى
وَيَسِّرْ لِىٓ أَمْرِى
وَاحْلُلْ عُقْدَةً مِّن لِّسَانِى
يَفْقَهُوا۟ قَوْلِى

Râbbish-râḥ lī ṣâdrī
wâ yâssir lī amrī
wâḥlûl 'uqdâtâm-mil-lisānī
yâfqâhū qawlī

"O my Lord! Expand me my breast: ease my task for me; and remove the impediment from my speech, so that they may understand what I say." (20:25-28)

---

(60) Sūrâh Al-Qaṣaṣ 28:24. Prayer of Prophet Mūsa عليه السلام when he reached Mâdyân tired, hungry and in desperate need of help.

(61) Sūrâh Tā-Hā 20:25-28. Prayer of Prophet Mūsa عليه السلام when he received Allāh's command in Sinai to go to the Pharaoh and point out his transgression.

III. Seeking the Protection of Allāh

(62)

سُبْحَٰنَكَ أَنتَ وَلِيُّنَا مِن دُونِهِم ۖ

Subḥānâkâ antâ wâliyyûnā min doonîhim

“Glory to Thee! Our (tie) is with Thee – as Protector – not with them.” (34:41)

(63)

حَسْبِيَ ٱللَّهُ لَآ إِلَٰهَ إِلَّا هُوَ ۖ عَلَيْهِ تَوَكَّلْتُ ۖ وَهُوَ رَبُّ ٱلْعَرْشِ ٱلْعَظِيمِ

Ḥâsbiyâl-lāhû lā-ilāhâ illāhu. ‘Alâyhi tâwwâkâltû wâhuwâ râbbul ‘ârshil ‘âẓeem

“Allāh sufficeth me: there is no god but He; on Him is my trust – He the Lord of the Throne (of Glory) Supreme!” (9:129)

(64)

رَبِّ إِنِّيٓ أَعُوذُ بِكَ أَنْ أَسْـَٔلَكَ مَا لَيْسَ لِي بِهِۦ عِلْمٌ ۖ
وَإِلَّا تَغْفِرْ لِي وَتَرْحَمْنِيٓ أَكُن مِّنَ ٱلْخَٰسِرِينَ

Râbbî innī a‘oodhû bikâ an âs’âlâkâ mā laysâ lī bihī ‘ilm
wâ’illā tâghfir-lī wâtârḥâmnī akûm-minâl khāsireen

---

(62) Sūrâh Saba’ 34:41. The response of the angels on the Day of Judgement when Allāh ﷻ asked them, ‘Was it you that these men used to worship?’

(63) Sūrâh At-Tawbah 9:129. Recitation of this du‘ā’ seven times in the morning and seven times in the evening is recommended by the Prophet ﷺ as a means of seeking the protection of Allāh from anything that worries us.

(64) Sūrâh Hūd 11:47. Prayer of Prophet Nūh عليه السلام when he was grieving for his unbelieving son who had drowned.

"O my Lord! I do seek refuge with Thee, lest I ask Thee for that of which I have no knowledge. And unless Thou forgive me and have mercy on me, I should indeed be lost!" (11:47)

(65)

فَاللَّهُ خَيْرٌ حَٰفِظًا ۖ وَهُوَ أَرْحَمُ الرَّٰحِمِينَ

Fâllāhû khâyrûn ḥāfiẓā. Wâhuwâ arḥâmûr-rāḥimeen

"But Allah is the best to take care (of him) and He is the Most Merciful of those who show mercy!" (12:64)

(66)

وَقُل رَّبِّ أَعُوذُ بِكَ مِنْ هَمَزَٰتِ الشَّيَٰطِينِ
وَأَعُوذُ بِكَ رَبِّ أَن يَحْضُرُونِ

Wâqûr-râbbî a'oodhû bikâ min hâmâzātish-shayāṭeen.
Wâ'a'oodhû bikâ râbbî ay-yâḥḍûroon

And say, "O my Lord! I seek refuge with Thee from the suggestions of the evil ones. And I seek refuge with Thee, O my Lord, lest they should come near me." (23: 97-98)

(67)

فَاطِرَ السَّمَٰوَٰتِ وَالْأَرْضِ أَنتَ وَلِىِّۦ فِى الدُّنْيَا
وَالْأَخِرَةِ ۖ تَوَفَّنِى مُسْلِمًا وَأَلْحِقْنِى بِالصَّٰلِحِينَ

Fāṭirâs-sâmāwātî wâl'ârḍî antâ wâlīyyī fid-dûnyā
wâl'ākhirâh. Tâwâffânī muslimaw-wâ'âlḥiqnī biṣṣāliḥeen

---

(65) Sūrâh Yūsuf 12:64. Prayer of Prophet Ya'qoob عليه السلام when his children asked him to send their younger brother (Bin Yamin) with them to Egypt to get more grain.

(66) Sūrâh Al-Mu'minūn 23:97-98

(67) Sūrâh Yūsuf 12:101. Prayer of Prophet Yūsuf عليه السلام after reuniting with his family.

"Creator of the heavens and the earth! Thou art my Protector in this world and in the Hereafter. Take Thou my soul (at death) as one submitting to Thy Will (as a Muslim) and unite me with the righteous." (12:101)

(68)

رَبَّنَا اصْرِفْ عَنَّا عَذَابَ جَهَنَّمَ ۖ إِنَّ عَذَابَهَا كَانَ غَرَامًا

Râbbânâṣrîf ‘annā ‘âdhābâ jâhânnâm innâ ‘âdhābâhā kānâ ghârāmā

"Our Lord! Avert from us the wrath of hell, for its wrath is indeed an affliction grievous." (25:65)

(69)

عَلَى اللَّهِ تَوَكَّلْنَا رَبَّنَا لَا تَجْعَلْنَا فِتْنَةً لِّلْقَوْمِ الظَّٰلِمِينَ
وَنَجِّنَا بِرَحْمَتِكَ مِنَ الْقَوْمِ الْكَٰفِرِينَ

‘Âlâl-lāhi tâwâkkâlnā. Râbbânā lā tâj‘âlnā fitnâtâl-lîlqawmîẓ-ẓalîmeen.
Wânâjjînā bîrâḥmâtikâ minâl qawmîl kāfîreen

"In Allāh do we put our trust. Our Lord! Make us not a trial for those who practise oppression. And deliver us by Thy Mercy from those who reject (Thee)." (10:85-86)

(70)

قُلْ أَعُوذُ بِرَبِّ الْفَلَقِ مِن شَرِّ مَا خَلَقَ وَمِن شَرِّ غَاسِقٍ إِذَا وَقَبَ
وَمِن شَرِّ النَّفَّٰثَٰتِ فِي الْعُقَدِ وَمِن شَرِّ حَاسِدٍ إِذَا حَسَدَ

Qul â‘oodhû bî râbbîl fâlâq. Min shârrî mā khâlâq. Wâmin shârrî ghāsiqîn idha wâqâb.
Wâmin shârrîn-nâffāthātî fil ‘ûqâd. Wâmin shârrî ḥāsidîn idhā ḥâsâd.

---

(68) Sūrâh Al-Furqān 25:65. Prayer of the righteous.

(69) Sūrâh Yūnus 10:85-86. Prayer of the followers of Mūsa عليه السلام in the face of Pharaoh's persecution.

Say: I seek refuge with the Lord of the Dawn; from the mischief of created things; from the mischief of darkness as it overspreads; from the mischief of those who practise secret arts and from the mischief of the envious one as he practises envy. (113:1-5)

(71)

قُلْ أَعُوذُ بِرَبِّ النَّاسِ مَلِكِ النَّاسِ إِلَٰهِ النَّاسِ
مِن شَرِّ الْوَسْوَاسِ الْخَنَّاسِ الَّذِى يُوَسْوِسُ
فِى صُدُورِ النَّاسِ مِنَ الْجِنَّةِ وَالنَّاسِ

Qul â'oodhû bî râbbîn-nās. Mâlîkîn-nās. Ilāhin-nās.
Min shârrîl wâwāsîl khânnās. Allâdhī yuwâswîsû
fī ṣûdūrīn-nās. Minâl jinnâtî wânnās.

Say: I seek refuge with the Lord and Cherisher of mankind; the King (or Ruler) of mankind; The God (or Judge) of mankind; from the mischief of the whisperer (of evil), who withdraws (after his whisper) – (the same) who whispers into the hearts of mankind, among jinns and among men. (114:1-6)

---

(70) Sūrâh Al-Fâlâq 113:1-5 and (71) Sūrâh An-Nās 114:1-6. Recitation of these Sūrâhs along with Sūrâh Al-Ikhlas (112), three times each is highly recommended in the morning and evening (for protection). (Abu Dawūd, At-Tirmidhi and An-Nasa'i)

IV. Offering of Thanks

(72)

بَلِ ٱللَّهَ فَٱعْبُدْ وَكُن مِّنَ ٱلشَّٰكِرِينَ

Bâlîl-lāhâ fa‘bûd wâkum minâsh-shākireen

Nay, but worship Allāh and be of those who give thanks. (39:66)

(73)

هَٰذَا مِن فَضْلِ رَبِّى لِيَبْلُوَنِىٓ ءَأَشْكُرُ أَمْ أَكْفُرُ ۖ وَمَن
شَكَرَ فَإِنَّمَا يَشْكُرُ لِنَفْسِهِۦ ۖ وَمَن كَفَرَ فَإِنَّ رَبِّى غَنِىٌّ كَرِيمٌ

Hādhā min fâḍlî râbbī liyâbluwânī a’ashkurû âm akfûr. Wâmân shâkârâ fâ’innâmā yâshkūrû linâfsih. Wâmân kâfârâ fâ’innâ râbbī ghânīyyun kâreem

"This is by the grace of my Lord! – To test me whether I am grateful or ungrateful! And if any is grateful, truly his gratitude is (a gain) for his own soul; but if any is ungrateful, truly my Lord is free of all needs, Supreme in Honour!" (27:40)

(74)

فَلِلَّهِ ٱلْحَمْدُ رَبِّ ٱلسَّمَٰوَٰتِ وَرَبِّ ٱلْأَرْضِ رَبِّ ٱلْعَٰلَمِينَ
وَلَهُ ٱلْكِبْرِيَآءُ فِى ٱلسَّمَٰوَٰتِ وَٱلْأَرْضِ ۖ وَهُوَ ٱلْعَزِيزُ ٱلْحَكِيمُ

Fâlillāhil ḥâmdû râbbis-sâmāwātî wârâbbil ’arḍî râbbil ‘ālâmeen. Wâlâhûl kibriā’û fis-sâmāwātî wâl’arḍ. Wâhuwâl ‘azīzul ḥâkeem

---

(72) Sūrâh Az-Zumâr 39:66

(73) Sūrâh An-Naml 27:40. Prayer of Prophet Sulaymān عليه السلام when he saw the throne of Bilqīs (Queen of Sheba) before him.

(74) Sūrâh Al-Jāthiyah 45:36-37

Then praise be to Allāh, Lord of the heavens and Lord of the earth. Lord and Cherisher of all the Worlds. To Him be glory throughout the heavens and the earth and He is Exalted in Power, full of Wisdom. (45:36-37)

(75)

ٱلْحَمْدُ لِلَّهِ ٱلَّذِى هَدَىٰنَا لِهَٰذَا وَمَا كُنَّا لِنَهْتَدِىَ لَوْلَآ أَنْ هَدَىٰنَا ٱللَّهُ ۖ

Alḥâmdulillāhil-lâdhī hadānā lihādhā wâmā kûnnā linâhtâdiyâ laulā ân hadānâl-lāh

Praise be to Allāh Who hath guided us to this (felicity); never could we have found guidance had it not been for the guidance of Allāh. (7:43)

(76)

وَهُوَ ٱللَّهُ لَآ إِلَٰهَ إِلَّا هُوَ ۖ لَهُ ٱلْحَمْدُ فِى ٱلْأُولَىٰ وَٱلْءَاخِرَةِ ۖ
وَلَهُ ٱلْحُكْمُ وَإِلَيْهِ تُرْجَعُونَ

Wâhûwallāhû lā-ilāha illāhu. Lâhûl ḥâmdû fîl oola wâl ākhîrâh.
Wâlâhûl ḥûkmû wâ'ilayhî turjâ'oon

And He is Allāh: there is no god but He. To Him be praise at the first and at the last; for Him is the Command and to Him shall ye (all) be brought back. (28:70)

(75) Sūrâh Al-A'rāf 7:43. A prayer of believers in Paradise who believed and worked righteousness.
(76) Sūrâh Al-Qaṣaṣ 28:70

V. Prayers for Family

(77)

رَبِّ لَا تَذَرْنِي فَرْدًا وَأَنتَ خَيْرُ الْوَارِثِينَ

Râbbî lā tâdhârnī fârdâw-wa'antâ khayrûl wāritheen

"O my Lord! Leave me not without offspring though Thou art the best of inheritors." (21:89)

(78)

رَبِّ هَبْ لِي مِنَ الصَّالِحِينَ

Râbbî hâblī mînâṣṣāliḥeen

"O my Lord! Grant me a righteous (son)!" (37:100)

(79)

رَبِّ هَبْ لِي مِن لَّدُنكَ ذُرِّيَّةً طَيِّبَةً ۖ إِنَّكَ سَمِيعُ الدُّعَاءِ

Râbbî hâblī mīllâdûnkâ dhûrriyâtân.tayyîbâtâh. Innâkâ sâmī 'ud-du'ā'

"O my Lord! Grant unto me from Thee a progeny that is pure: for Thou art He that heareth prayer!" (3:38)

---

(77) Sūrâh Al-Anbiyā' 21:89. Prayer of Prophet Zâkâriyyā عليه السلام expressing his desire to have a son. He was blessed with Yâḥyā.

(78) Sūrâh As-Ṣāffāt 37:100. Prayer of Prophet Ibrāhīm عليه السلام.

(79) Sūrâh Āli-'Imrān 3:38. Prayer of Prophet Zâkâriyyā عليه السلام.

(80)

رَبَّنَا هَبْ لَنَا مِنْ أَزْوَاجِنَا وَذُرِّيَّتِنَا
قُرَّةَ أَعْيُنٍ وَاجْعَلْنَا لِلْمُتَّقِينَ إِمَامًا

Râbbânā hâblânā mîn azwājînā wâdhûrriyātînā
qûrrâtâ a'yuniw wâj'alnā lîl mûttâqeenâ imāmā

"Our Lord! Grant unto us wives and offspring who will be the comfort of our eyes and give us (the grace) to lead the righteous." (25:74)

(81)

رَبَّنَا وَاجْعَلْنَا مُسْلِمَيْنِ لَكَ وَمِن ذُرِّيَّتِنَا أُمَّةً مُّسْلِمَةً لَّكَ
وَأَرِنَا مَنَاسِكَنَا وَتُبْ عَلَيْنَآ إِنَّكَ أَنتَ التَّوَّابُ الرَّحِيمُ

Râbbânā wâj'alnā muslimaynî lâkâ wâmin dhûrriyâtînā ummâtâm-muslimâtâl-lâkâ
wâ'arînā mânāsîkânā wâtûb 'alaynā innâkâ antât-tâwwābûr-râḥeem

"Our Lord! Make of us Muslims, bowing to Thy (Will) and of our progeny a people Muslim, bowing to Thy (Will); And show us our places for the celebration of (due) rites; and turn to us (in Mercy); for Thou are the Oft-Returning, Most Merciful." (2:128)

(82)

رَبِّ اجْعَلْنِى مُقِيمَ الصَّلَوٰةِ وَمِن ذُرِّيَّتِى رَبَّنَا وَتَقَبَّلْ دُعَآءِ
رَبَّنَا اغْفِرْلِى وَلِوَٰلِدَىَّ وَلِلْمُؤْمِنِينَ يَوْمَ يَقُومُ الْحِسَابُ

Râbbîj 'âlnī muqeemâs-ṣâlātî wâmin dhûrrîyâtī. Râbbânā wâtâqâbbâl du'ā'.
Râbbânâghfîrlī wâliwālidayyâ wâ lîl mu'mineenâ yawmâ yâqoomûl ḥisāb

---

(80) Sūrâh Al-Furqān 25:74

(81) Sūrâh Al-Bâqârâh 2:128

(82) Sūrâh Ibrāhīm 14:40-41. Prayer of Prophet Ibrāhīm عليه السلام.

"O my Lord! Make me one who establishes regular prayer and also (raise such) among my offspring. O our Lord! And accept Thou my prayer. O our Lord! Cover (us) with Thy forgiveness – me, my parents and (all) believers – on the Day that the Reckoning will be established!" (14:40-41)

(83)

رَبِّ أَوْزِعْنِىٓ أَنْ أَشْكُرَ نِعْمَتَكَ ٱلَّتِىٓ أَنْعَمْتَ عَلَىَّ وَعَلَىٰ وَٰلِدَىَّ وَأَنْ أَعْمَلَ صَٰلِحًا تَرْضَىٰهُ وَأَصْلِحْ لِى فِى ذُرِّيَّتِىٓ ۖ إِنِّى تُبْتُ إِلَيْكَ وَإِنِّى مِنَ ٱلْمُسْلِمِينَ

Râbbî 'awzi'nī ân âshkûrâ ni'mâtâkâl lâtī ân'amtâ 'alayyâ wâ'âlā wālidayyâ wâ'ân a'mâlâ ṣālihân târdāhû wâ'aṣlîḥ-lī fī dhurrîyâtī. Innī tûbtû ilaykâ wâ'innī minâl muslimeen

"O my Lord! Grant me that I may be grateful for Thy favour which Thou hast bestowed upon me and upon both my parents and that I may work righteousness such as Thou mayest approve and be gracious to me in my issue. Truly have I turned to Thee and truly do I bow (to Thee) in Islam." (46:15)

(84)

رَّبِّ ٱرْحَمْهُمَا كَمَا رَبَّيَانِى صَغِيرًا

Râbbîr-ḥâmhûmā kâmā râbbâyānī ṣâgheerā

"My Lord! Bestow on them Thy Mercy even as they cherished me in childhood." (17:24)

---

(83) Sūrâh Al-Aḥqāf 46:15. Prayer of the believer upon reaching the age of 40.

(84) Sūrâh Al-Isrā' 17:24. Prayer for parents.

(85)

رَّبِّ اغْفِرْلِى وَلِوَٰلِدَىَّ وَلِمَن دَخَلَ بَيْتِىَ مُؤْمِنًا
وَلِلْمُؤْمِنِينَ وَالْمُؤْمِنَٰتِ وَلَا تَزِدِ الظَّٰلِمِينَ إِلَّا تَبَارًا

Râbbîghfirlī wâliwālîdayyâ wâlimân dâkhâlâ baytiyâ mu'minaw-wâlil mu'mineenâ wâl mu'mināti wâlā tazidiẓ-ẓālimeenâ illā tâbārā

"O my Lord! Forgive me, my parents, all those who enter my house in faith and (all) believing men and believing women and to the wrong doers grant Thou no increase but in perdition." (71:28)

---

(85) Sūrâh Nūḥ 71:28. Prayer of Prophet Nūḥ عليه السلام.

VI. General

(86)

رَبَّنَا آتِنَا فِي الدُّنْيَا حَسَنَةً وَفِي الْآخِرَةِ حَسَنَةً
وَقِنَا عَذَابَ النَّارِ

Râbbânā ātînā fîd-dûnyā ḥâsânâtâw-wâfil ākhîrâtî ḥâsânâtâw-wâqînā 'adhābân-nār

"Our Lord! Give us good in this world and good in the Hereafter and defend us from the torment of the Fire!" (2:201)

(87)

وَاكْتُبْ لَنَا فِي هَٰذِهِ الدُّنْيَا حَسَنَةً وَفِي الْآخِرَةِ
إِنَّا هُدْنَا إِلَيْكَ

Wâktûb lânā fī hādhîhîd-dûnyā ḥâsânâtâw wâfil ākhîrâtî innā hûdnā ilayk

"And ordain for us that which is good in this life and in the Hereafter: for we have turned unto Thee." (7:156)

---

(86) Sūrâh Al-Bâqârâh 2:201

(87) Sūrâh Al-A'rāf 7:156. Prayer of Prophet Mūsa عليه السلام after rebuking the Israelites for their backsliding into idolatry.

(88)

قَدِ افْتَرَيْنَا عَلَى اللَّهِ كَذِبًا إِنْ عُدْنَا فِي مِلَّتِكُم بَعْدَ إِذْ
نَجَّىٰنَا اللَّهُ مِنْهَا ۚ وَمَا يَكُونُ لَنَآ أَن نَّعُودَ فِيهَآ إِلَّآ أَن يَشَآءَ
اللَّهُ رَبُّنَا ۚ وَسِعَ رَبُّنَا كُلَّ شَيْءٍ عِلْمًا ۚ عَلَى اللَّهِ تَوَكَّلْنَا ۚ
رَبَّنَا افْتَحْ بَيْنَنَا وَبَيْنَ قَوْمِنَا بِالْحَقِّ وَأَنتَ خَيْرُ الْفَٰتِحِينَ

Qâdîf târaynā 'âlâllāhi kâdhîbân in 'ûdnā fī millâtîkum bâ'dâ idh nâjjānâl-lāhû minhā. Wâmā yâkoonû lânā ân nâ'ūdâ fīhā illā ay-yâshā'â âllāhû râbbûnā. Wâsi'â râbbûnā kûllâ shay'în 'ilmā 'âlâllāhî tâwâkkâlnā. Râbbânâftâḥ baynânâ wâbaynâ qawmînā bilḥâqqi wâ'antâ khayrûl fātiḥeen

"We should indeed invent a lie against Allāh if we returned to your ways after Allāh hath rescued us therefrom; nor could we by any manner of means return thereto unless it be as in the will and plan of Allāh, our Lord. Our Lord can reach out to the utmost recesses of things by His knowledge. In Allāh is our trust. Our Lord! Decide Thou between us and our people in truth for Thou art the best to decide." (7:89)

(89)

رَبَّنَا وَسِعْتَ كُلَّ شَيْءٍ رَّحْمَةً وَعِلْمًا فَاغْفِرْ لِلَّذِينَ
تَابُوا وَاتَّبَعُوا سَبِيلَكَ وَقِهِمْ عَذَابَ الْجَحِيمِ
رَبَّنَا وَأَدْخِلْهُمْ جَنَّٰتِ عَدْنٍ الَّتِي وَعَدتَّهُمْ وَمَن صَلَحَ مِنْ
ءَابَآئِهِمْ وَأَزْوَٰجِهِمْ وَذُرِّيَّٰتِهِمْ ۚ إِنَّكَ أَنتَ الْعَزِيزُ الْحَكِيمُ

---

(88) Sūrâh Al-A'râf 7:89. Response of the people of Prophet Shu'ayb ﷺ when they were threatened by their countrymen.

(89) Sūrâh Ghāfir 40:7-9. Prayer of the angels on behalf of the believers.

وَقِهِمُ السَّيِّئَاتِ ۚ وَمَن تَقِ السَّيِّئَاتِ يَوْمَئِذٍ
فَقَدْ رَحِمْتَهُ ۚ وَذَٰلِكَ هُوَ الْفَوْزُ الْعَظِيمُ

Râbbânā wâsî'tâ kullâ shay'ir-raḥmâtâw-wâ 'ilmân fâghfir lîllâdhīnâ tābū wâttâbâ'oo sâbīlâkâ wâqîhîm 'adhābâl jâḥeem. Râbbânā wâ'adkhîlhûm jânnāti 'âdnîllâtī wâ'adtâhûm wâmân ṣâlâḥâ min ābā'ihîm wâ'azwājihîm wâdhûrriyātîhîm. Innâkâ ântâl 'azīzûl ḥâkeem. Wâqîhîmûs-sayyi'āt. Wâmân tâqis-sayyi'ātî yawmâ'idhîn fâqâd râḥimtâh. Wâdhālikâ hûwâl fawzûl 'âẓeem

"Our Lord! Thy reach is over all things in Mercy and Knowledge. Forgive, then, those who turn in repentance and follow Thy path and preserve them from the penalty of the blazing fire. And grant, Our Lord, that they enter the Gardens of Eternity which Thou hast promised to them and to the righteous among their fathers, their wives and their posterity! For Thou art (He) the Exalted in Might, full of wisdom. And preserve them from (all) ills and any whom Thou dost preserve from ills that Day – on them wilt Thou have bestowed mercy indeed; and that will be truly (for them) the highest achievment." (40:7-9)

Chapter Two:

Du‘ā’ from Sunnah:
Al-Ma’thūrāt

(90)

أَصْبَحْنَا وَأَصْبَحَ الْمُلْكُ لِلَّهِ وَالْحَمْدُ لِلَّهِ لَا شَرِيكَ

لَهُ ، لَا إِلَهَ إِلَّا هُوَ وَإِلَيْهِ النُّشُورُ (ثلاثاً)

Aṣbâḥnā wâ'aṣbâḥâl mulkû lillāhi wâlḥâmdûlillāhi lā shârīkâ
lâhū lā ilāha illā hûwâ wâ'ilayhîn-nûshoor

We rose up in the morning and so does the domain of Allāh's. Grace is due to Him, He has no partner. There is no deity but Him, unto Whom is the return. (3 times)

(91)

أَصْبَحْنَا عَلَى فِطْرَةِ الْإِسْلَامِ ، وَكَلِمَةِ الْإِخْلَاصِ وَعَلَى

دِينِ نَبِيِّنَا مُحَمَّدٍ صَلَّى اللَّهُ عَلَيْهِ وَسَلَّمَ ، وَعَلَى مِلَّةِ

أَبِينَا إِبْرَاهِيمَ حَنِيفاً وَمَا كَانَ مِنَ الْمُشْرِكِينَ (ثلاثاً)

Aṣbâḥnā 'alā fitrâtîl islāmî wâkâlîmâtil ikhlāṣî wâ 'alā
deenî nâbiyyinā Muḥâmmâdin ṣâllâllāhû 'alayhi wâsâllâm wâ 'alā mîllâtî
abīnā Ibrāhīmâ ḥânifâw-wâmā kānâ minâl mushrikeen

We rose up with the innate nature of *Al-Islām* and with the word of purity (*Ikhlās*) and on the way of life (*deen*) of our Prophet Muḥâmmâd ﷺ and on the *deen* of our father Ibrāhīm عليه السلام, the upright (in truth) who was not of the *mushriks* (associators of other deities with Allāh). (3 times)

---

(90) Ibn-us-Sunni, Al-Bazzar. In the evening the word *aṣbaḥna* is changed to *amsayna* (we begin the evening) and the word *aṣbaḥa* is changed to *amsa*.

(91) Abdullah bin Imam Ahmad. In the evening the word *aṣbaḥna* is changed to *amsayna*.

(92)

اَللّٰهُمَّ إِنِّى أَصْبَحْتُ مِنْكَ فِى نِعْمَةٍ وَعَافِيَةٍ وَسِتْرٍ، فَأَتِمَّ
عَلَيَّ نِعْمَتَكَ وَعَافِيَتَكَ وَسِتْرَكَ فِى الدُّنْيَا وَالْآخِرَةِ (ثلاثاً)

Allāhûmmâ innī aṣbâḥtû minkâ fī ni'mâtiw-wâ 'āfiyâtiw-wâsîtrin fâ'atimmâ 'alayyâ ni'mâtâkâ wâ 'āfiyâtâkâ wâsîtrâkâ fīd-dûnyā wâl ākhirâh

O Allāh! I rose up in the morning with blessings, strength and concealment (of my deficiencies), all from You. So complete all the blessings and strength from You and the concealment for me in this life and in the Hereafter. (3 times)

(93)

اَللّٰهُمَّ مَا أَصْبَحَ بِى مِنْ نِعْمَةٍ أَوْ بِأَحَدٍ مِنْ خَلْقِكَ فَمِنْكَ
وَحْدَكَ لَا شَرِيكَ لَكَ، فَلَكَ الْحَمْدُ، وَلَكَ الشُّكْرُ (ثلاثاً)

Allāhûmmâ mā aṣbâḥâ bī min ni'mâtin au bî'aḥâdîn min khâlqîkâ fâminkâ wâḥdâkâ lā shârīkâ lâkâ fâlâkâl ḥâmdû wâlâkâsh-shukr

O Allāh! Whatever blessings I or any of Your creatures rose up with are only from You, You have no partner, so all grace and thanks are due to You. (3 times)

(94)

يَا رَبِّى لَكَ الْحَمْدُ كَمَا يَنْبَغِى لِجَلَالِ وَجْهِكَ وَعَظِيمِ
سُلْطَانِكَ (ثلاثاً)

Yā râbbī lâkâl ḥâmdû kâmā yânbâghī lījâlālî wâjhikâ wâ 'aẓeemî sulṭānik

---

(92) Ibn-us-Sunni. In the evening the word *aṣbaḥtu* is changed to *amsaytu*.

(93) Abu Dawūd, An-Nasā'i and Ibn Ḥibbān. In the evening the word *aṣbaḥa* is changed to *amsa*.

(94) Aḥmad and Ibn Majah

O my Lord! All grace is due to You which is befitting to Your glorious presence and Your great sovereignty. (3 times)

(95)

رَضِيتُ بِاللهِ رَبًّا ، وَبِالْإِسْلَامِ دِينًا ، وَبِمُحَمَّدٍ نَبِيًّا وَرَسُولاً (ثلاثاً)

Raḍitû billāhi râbbā wâ bil islāmî dīnā wâ bîmuḥâmmâdîn nâbiyyaw-wâ râsoolā

I have accepted Allāh for Lord, *al-Islām* as a way of life and Muḥâmmâd ﷺ Prophet and Messenger of Allāh. (3 times)

(96)

سُبْحَانَ اللهِ وَبِحَمْدِهِ ، عَدَدَ خَلْقِهِ وَرِضَا نَفْسِهِ ، وَزِنَةَ عَرْشِهِ ، وَمِدَادَ كَلِمَاتِهِ (ثلاثاً)

Subḥānâllāhi wâbiḥâmdihi 'adâdâ khâlqîhi wârîḍā nâfsihi wâzînâtâ 'arshihi wâmidādâ kâlimātih

Glory be to Allāh and grace is His (as great as) the number of His creatures, the extent of His satisfaction, the weight of His domain and the ink (needed to write down His countless) signs (of presence, omnipotence and grace). (3 times)

(95) Abu Dawūd, At-Tirmidhi, An-Nasā'i and Al-Ḥakim

(96) Muslim. Highly rewarded du'ā'.

(97)

بِسْمِ اللَّهِ الَّذِي لَا يَضُرُّ مَعَ اسْمِهِ شَيْءٌ فِي الْأَرْضِ
وَلَا فِي السَّمَاءِ وَهُوَ السَّمِيعُ الْعَلِيمُ (ثلاثاً)

Bismillāhil lâdhī lā yâḍûrrû ma'âsmihi shay'ûn fil arḍi
wâlā fis samā'î wâhuwâs sâmī'ul 'aleem

In the name of Allāh, with Whose name nothing on earth or in the heavens can harm and He is the Hearer, the Knower. (3 times)

(98)

اللَّهُمَّ إِنَّا نَعُوذُ بِكَ مِنْ أَنْ نُشْرِكَ بِكَ شَيْئًا
نَعْلَمُهُ، وَنَسْتَغْفِرُكَ لِمَا لَا نَعْلَمُهُ (ثلاثاً)

Allāhûmmâ innā na'oodhû bîkâ min ân-nûshrîkâ bîkâ shay'ân
na'lâmûhu wânâstâghfirûkâ lîmā lā na'lâmûh

O Allāh! We seek Your refuge from knowingly associating others with You and we seek Your forgiveness from associating others with You unknowingly. (3 times)

(99)

أَعُوذُ بِكَلِمَاتِ اللَّهِ التَّامَّاتِ مِنْ شَرِّ مَا خَلَقَ (ثلاثاً)

Ā'oodhû bîkâlîmātîl lāhît-tāmmātî min shârrî mā khâlâq

I seek refuge in the perfect words of Allāh from any evil creature. (3 times)

---

(97) Abu Dawūd and At-Tirmidhi. Excellent du'ā' for seeking the protection of Allāh.

(98) Aḥmad and Aṭ-Tâbarani

(99) Ibn Ḥibbān

(100)

اللَّهُمَّ إِنِّي أَعُوذُ بِكَ مِنَ الْهَمِّ وَالْحَزَنِ ، وأعوذ بك
مِنَ الْعَجْزِ وَالْكَسَلِ ، وَأَعُوذُ بِكَ مِنَ الْجُبْنِ وَالْبُخْلِ ،
وَأَعُوذُ بِكَ مِنْ غَلَبَةِ الدَّيْنِ وَقَهْرِ الرِّجَالِ (ثلاثاً)

Allāhûmmâ innī ā'oodhû bîkâ minâl hâmmî wâl hâzânî wâ ā'oodhû bîkâ minâl 'ajzî wâl kâsâlî wâ ā'oodhû bîkâ minâl jûbnî wâl bukhlî wâ ā'oodhû bîkâ min ghâlâbâtîd-daynî wâqahrîr-rijāl

O Allāh! I seek refuge in You from worry and grief, from helplessness and laziness, from cowardice and stinginess and from overpowering of debt and from oppression of men. (3 times)

(101)

اللَّهُمَّ عَافِنِي فِي بَدَنِي ، اللَّهُمَّ عافِنِي فِي سَمْعِي ،
اللَّهُمَّ عافِنِي فِي بَصَرِي (ثلاثاً)

Allāhûmmâ 'āfinī fī bâdânī allāhûmmâ 'āfinī fī sâm'ī allāhûmmâ 'āfinī fī bâṣârī

O Allāh! Grant health to my body, to my hearing and to my sight. (3 times)

---

(100) Abu Dawūd. Excellent du'ā' for worry or debt.

(101) Abu Dawūd

(102)

اَللّٰهُمَّ إِنِّي أَعُوذُ بِكَ مِنَ الْكُفْرِ وَالْفَقْرِ ، اَللّٰهُمَّ إِنِّي
أَعُوذُ بِكَ مِنْ عَذَابِ الْقَبْرِ ، لَا إِلٰهَ إِلَّا أَنْتَ (ثلاثًا)

Allāhûmmâ innī ā'oodhû bîkâ minâl kûfrî wâl fâqrî allāhûmmâ innī ā'oodhû bîkâ min 'adhābil qâbrî lā illāha illā'ant

O Allāh! I seek refuge in You from unbelief and poverty. O Allāh! I seek refuge in You from the punishment of the grave. There is no deity but You. (3 times)

(103)

اَللّٰهُمَّ أَنْتَ رَبِّي لَا إِلٰهَ إِلَّا أَنْتَ ، خَلَقْتَنِي وَأَنَا عَبْدُكَ
وَأَنَا عَلَى عَهْدِكَ وَوَعْدِكَ مَا اسْتَطَعْتُ ، أَعُوذُ بِكَ مِنْ
شَرِّ مَا صَنَعْتُ ، أَبُوءُ لَكَ بِنِعْمَتِكَ عَلَيَّ وَأَبُوءُ بِذَنْبِي
فَاغْفِرْ لِي فَإِنَّهُ لَا يَغْفِرُ الذُّنُوبَ إِلَّا أَنْتَ (ثلاثًا)

Allāhûmmâ ântâ râbbī lā illāha illā'ant khâlâqtânī wâ'anā 'abdûkâ wâ'anā 'alā 'ahdîkâ wâwa'dîkâ mâstạta'tû ā'oodhû bîkâ min shârrî mā ṣana'tû aboo'û lâkâ bîni'mâtikâ 'alayyâ wa'aboo'û bîdhânbī fâghfîrlī fa'innâhū lā yâghfîrûdh-dhûnoobâ illā ant

O Allāh! You are my Lord, there is no deity but You. You created me and I am Your slave-servant and I am trying my best to keep my oath (of faith) to You and to seek to live in the hope of Your promise. I seek refuge in You from my greatest evil deeds. I acknowledge Your blessings upon me and I acknowledge my sins, so forgive me for none but You can forgive sins. (3 times)

---

(102) Abu Dawūd

(103) Al-Bukhāri. The Prophet ﷺ called this 'the master du'ā' for seeking forgiveness'.

(104)

أَسْتَغْفِرُ اللّٰهَ الَّذِى لَا إِلٰهَ إِلَّا هُوَ الْحَىَّ الْقَيُّومَ
وَأَتُوبُ إِلَيْهِ (ثَلَاثًا)

Astâghfirûl lāhâl lâdhī lā ilāha illā huwâl hâyyâl qâyyūmâ wa'atoobû ilayh

I seek forgiveness from Allāh, there is no deity but Him, the Living, the Eternal and I repent to Him. (3 times)

(105)

اَللّٰهُمَّ صَلِّ عَلَى سَيِّدِنَا مُحَمَّدٍ وَعَلَى آلِ سَيِّدِنَا مُحَمَّدٍ
كَمَا صَلَّيْتَ عَلَى سَيِّدِنَا إِبْرَاهِيمَ وَعَلَى آلِ سَيِّدِنَا إِبْرَاهِيمَ
وَبَارِكْ عَلَى سَيِّدِنَا مُحَمَّدٍ وَعَلَى آلِ سَيِّدِنَا مُحَمَّدٍ كَمَا
بَارَكْتَ عَلَى سَيِّدِنَا إِبْرَاهِيمَ وَعَلَى آلِ سَيِّدِنَا إِبْرَاهِيمَ
فِى الْعَالَمِينَ ، إِنَّكَ حَمِيدٌ مَجِيدٌ (عَشْرًا)

Allāhûmmâ ṣâllī 'alā sayyîdînā Muḥâmmâdiw-wâ 'alā ālî sayyîdînā Muḥâmmâdin kâmā ṣâllaytâ 'alā sayyîdînā Ibrāhīmâ wâ 'alā ālî sayyîdînā Ibrāhīmâ wâ bārîk 'alā sayyîdînā Muḥâmmâdiw-wâ 'alā ālî sayyîdînā Muḥâmmâdin kâmā bārâktâ 'alā sayyîdînā Ibrāhīmâ wâ 'alā ālî sayyîdînā Ibrāhīmâ fil 'ālâmīnâ innâkâ ḥâmīdum-mâjīd

O Allāh! Have mercy on Muḥâmmâd ﷺ and on the progeny of Muḥâmmâd ﷺ, as you had mercy on Ibrāhīm عليه السلام and the progeny of Ibrāhīm عليه السلام and bless Muḥâmmâd ﷺ and the progeny of Muḥâmmâd ﷺ, as you blessed Ibrāhīm عليه السلام and the progeny of Ibrāhīm عليه السلام in this universe. Indeed You are Gracious, Glorious. (10 times)

---

(104) Abu Dawūd, At-Tirmidhi and Al-Ḥakim

(105) Aṭ-Ṭabarani

(106)

سُبُحَانَ اللّٰهِ، وَالْحَمدُ لِلّٰهِ، وَلَا إِلَهَ إِلَّا اللّٰهُ، وَاللّٰهُ أَكبَرُ (مِائة)

Subḥānâllāh wâl ḥâmdûlillāh wâ lā-ilāhâ illâllāhû wâllāhû âkbâr

Glory be to Allāh, grace is due to Allāh, there is no deity but Allāh and Allāh is The Great. (100 times)

(107)

لَا إِلَهَ إِلَّا اللّٰهُ وَحْدَهُ لَا شَرِيكَ لَهُ، لَهُ الْمُلْكُ وَلَهُ الْحَمدُ، وَهُوَ عَلَى كُلِّ شَيْءٍ قَدِيرٌ (عَشراً)

Lā-ilāhâ illâllāhû wāḥdâhū lā shârīkâ lâhū lâhûl mûlkû wâ lâhûl ḥâmd wâhuwâ 'alā kullî shay'in qâdeer

There is no deity but Allāh alone; He has no partner. Sovereignty and grace are His and He is Omnipotent. (10 times)

(108)

سُبُحَانَكَ اللَّهُمَّ وَبِحَمْدِكَ، أَشْهَدُ أَنْ لَا إِلَهَ إِلَّا أَنْتَ، أَسْتَغْفِرُكَ وَأَتُوبُ إِلَيْكَ (ثلاثاً)

Subḥānâkâllāhûmmâ wâbîḥâmdikâ ash-hâdû allā ilāha illā 'antâ âstâghfirûkâ wâ 'atoobû ilayk

Glory be to You, O Allāh and all praise! I testify that there is no deity but You. I seek Your forgiveness and to You do I repent. (3 times)

---

(106) At-Tirmidhi

(107) Ahmad and Aṭ-Ṭabarani. This du'ā' is recommended after Fajr and Maghrib prayers.

(108) An-Nasā'i, Aṭ-Ṭabarani and Al-Ḥakim. This du'ā' is recommended at the end of meetings. It atones for one's infractions during the meeting.

Chapter Three:

Daily Du‘ā’

Waking up

(109)

الْحَمْدُ لِلَّهِ الَّذِي أَحْيَانَا بَعْدَ مَا أَمَاتَنَا وَإِلَيْهِ النُّشُورُ

Alḥâmdûlillāhil lâdhī aḥyānā ba'dâmā amātânā wâ'ilayhîn-nûshoor

Praise be to Allāh Who gave us life after death and unto Whom will be the return.

When entering the bathroom

(110)

اللَّهُمَّ إِنِّي أَعُوذُ بِكَ مِنَ الْخُبُثِ وَالْخَبَائِثِ

Allāhûmmâ innī a'oodhû bîkâ minâl khûbthî wâl khâbā'ith

O Allāh! I seek refuge in You from male and female devils.

When leaving the bathroom

(111)

غُفْرَانَكَ

Ghûfrānâkâ

I seek Your forgiveness (O Allāh!)

---

(109) Al-Bukhāri

(110) Al-Bukhāri and Muslim

(111) Abu Dawūd

While making Wuḍū' (ablution)

(112)

اَللّٰهُمَّ اغْفِرْلِىْ ذَنْبِىْ وَوَسِّعْ لِىْ فِىْ دَارِىْ وَبَارِكْ لِىْ فِىْ رِزْقِىْ

Allāhûmmâghfirlī dhânbī wâwâssi'lī fī dārī wâbārīklī fī rizqī

O Allāh! Forgive my sins and expand (bless) my home and bless my livelihood.

After completing Wuḍū'

(113)

أَشْهَدُ أَنْ لَا إِلٰهَ إِلَّا اللّٰهُ وَحْدَهُ لَا شَرِيكَ لَهُ ،
وَأَشْهَدُ أَنَّ مُحَمَّداً عَبْدُهُ وَرَسُولُهُ ، اَللّٰهُمَّ
اجْعَلْنِى مِنَ التَّوَّابِينَ ، وَاجْعَلْنِى مِنَ الْمُتَطَهِّرِينَ

Ash-hâdû allā ilāha illâllāhû wāḥdâhu lā shârīkâ lâhu
wâ ash-hâdû ânnâ Muḥâmmâdân 'abdûhû wârâsoolûh. Allāhûmmâj
'alnī minât tâwwābīna wâj 'alnī minâl mutâṭahhirīn

I bear witness that there is no deity but Allāh; He is alone. He has no partner. And I bear witness that Muḥâmmâd ﷺ is His servant and Messenger. O Allāh! Make me of those who are repentant and of those who purify themselves.

---

(112) An-Nasā'i

(113) Muslim and At-Tirmidhi

After Adhān is complete

(114)

اللَّهُمَّ رَبَّ هٰذِهِ الدَّعْوَةِ التَّامَّةِ، وَالصَّلَاةِ الْقَائِمَةِ آتِ مُحَمَّدًا الْوَسِيلَةَ وَالْفَضِيلَةَ، وَابْعَثْهُ مَقَامًا مَحْمُودًا الَّذِى وَعَدْتَهُ

Allāhûmmâ rābbâ hādhîhîd-da‘wâtît tāmmâtî wâṣ-ṣalātîl qā’imâtî ātî Muḥâmmâdâl wasīlâtâ wâl fâḍîlâtâ. Wâb‘ath-hû mâqāmân mâḥmūdâl-lâdhī wâ‘adtâh

O Allāh! Lord of this perfect call and the *ṣalāh* to be offered, grant Muḥâmmâd 🕌 the privilege (of interceding) and also the eminence and resurrect him to the praised position You have promised.

When leaving the house

(115)

بِسْمِ اللّٰهِ تَوَكَّلْتُ عَلَى اللّٰهِ وَلَاحَوْلَ وَلَا قُوَّةَ إِلَّا بِاللّٰهِ

Bismillāhi tâwâkkâltû ‘alâllāhî wâlâ ḥawlâ wâlâ qūwwâtâ illā billāh

In the name of Allāh. I depend on Allāh. There is no ability or power (for us) except by the leave of Allāh.

---

(114) Al-Bukhāri
(115) Abu Dawūd, At-Tirmidhi and An-Nasā'i

When going to the Mâsjid (mosque)

(116)

اللّٰهُمَّ اجْعَلْ فِي قَلْبِي نُورًا ، وَفِي بَصَرِي نُورًا ،
وَفِي سَمْعِي نُورًا ، وَعَنْ يَمِينِي نُورًا ، وَعَنْ يَسَارِي
نُورًا ، وَفَوْقِي نُورًا ، وَتَحْتِي نُورًا ، وَأَمَامِي نُورًا ،
وَخَلْفِي نُورًا ، وَاجْعَلْ لِي نُورًا

Allāhûmmâj 'al fī qalbī nooran wâfī bâṣârī nooran
wâfī sam'ī nooran wâ'an yâmīnī nooran wâ'an yâsārī
nooran wâ fawqī nooran wâ tâḥtī nooran wâ'amāmī nooran
wâ khâlfī nooran wâj'al-lī nooran

O Allāh! Grant me light in my heart, light in my sight, light in my hearing, light to my right, light to my left, light above me, light underneath me, light before me, light behind me and grant me light.

When entering the Mâsjid

(117)

بِسْمِ اللّٰهِ اللّٰهُمَّ صَلِّ عَلَى مُحَمَّدٍ اللّٰهُمَّ افْتَحْ لِي أَبْوَابَ رَحْمَتِكَ

Bismillāh allāhûmmâ ṣalli 'alā Muḥâmmâdin allāhûmmâftâḥ lī âbwābâ râḥmâtikâ

In the name of Allāh. O Allāh! Bless Muḥâmmâd ﷺ. O Allāh! Open Your gates of mercy for me.

---

(116) Al-Bukhāri

(117) Muslim, Abu Dawūd and An-Nasā'i

After completing Ṣalāh

(118)

سُبۡحَٰنَ ٱللَّهِ ٱلۡحَمۡدُ لِلَّهِ ٱللَّهُ أَكۡبَر

لَا إِلَٰهَ إِلَّا ٱللَّهُ وَحۡدَهُ لَا شَرِيكَ لَهُ، لَهُ ٱلۡمُلۡكُ وَلَهُ ٱلۡحَمۡدُ

وَهُوَ عَلَىٰ كُلِّ شَيۡءٍ قَدِيرٌ

Sûbhānallāh (33 times); *Alhâmdulillāh* (33 times); *Allāhu Akbâr* (33 times); *Lā-ilāhâ illâllāhû wāḥdâhū lā shârīkâ lâhū lâhûl mûlkû wâ lâhûl ḥâmd wâhuwâ 'alā kullî shay'in qâdeer*

Glory be to Allah (33 times); Praise be to Allah (33 times); Allah is Great (33 times). There is no deity but Allah alone; He has no partner. Sovereignty and grace are His and He is Omnipotent.

When leaving the Mâsjid

(119)

ٱللَّهُمَّ إِنِّىٓ أَسۡئَلُكَ مِنۡ فَضۡلِكَ

Allāhûmmâ innī as'alûkâ mîn faḍlikâ

O Allah! I beg of You Your bounty

---

(118) Muslim

(119) Muslim, Abu Dawūd and An-Nasā'i

When entering the house

(120)

اَللّٰهُمَّ إِنِّي أَسْأَلُكَ خَيْرَ الْمَوْلِجِ وَخَيْرَ الْمَخْرَجِ ، بِاسْمِ اللّٰهِ وَلَجْنَا ، وَبِاسْمِ اللّٰهِ خَرَجْنَا وَعَلَى اللّٰهِ رَبِّنَا تَوَكَّلْنَا ، ثُمَّ لِيُسَلِّمْ عَلَى أَهْلِهِ

Allāhûmmâ innī as'alûkâ khâyrâl mawlîjî wâ khâyrâl mâkhrâjî bismillāhi wâlâjnā wâ bismillāhi khârâjnā wâ 'alâllāhi râbbînā tâwâkkâlnā (then offer salām on the family)

O Allāh! I ask you (to grant me) the best entering and the best exit. In the name of Allāh we entered and in the name of Allāh we left and upon Allāh our Lord we depend (then offer *salām* on the family).

When beginning the meal

(121)

اَللّٰهُمَّ بَارِكْ لَنَا فِيمَا رَزَقْتَنَا ، وَقِنَا عَذَابَ النَّارِ ، بِسْمِ اللّٰهِ

Allāhûmmâ bārik lânā fīmā râzâqtânā wâqinā adhābân-nār. Bismillāh.

O Allāh! Bless (the food) You provided us and save us from the punishment of the hellfire. In the name of Allāh.

---

(120) Abu Dawūd

(121) Ibn-us-Sunni

When finishing the meal

(122)

الْحَمْدُ لِلّٰهِ الَّذِى أَطْعَمَنَا وَسَقَانَا وَجَعَلَنَا مُسْلِمِينَ

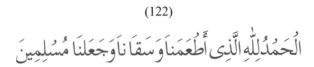

Alḥâmdûlillāhi lâdhī aṭ'amânā wâsâqānā wâja'alnā muslimeen

Praise be to Allāh Who has fed us and given us drink and made us Muslims.

While undressing

(123)

بِسْمِ اللّٰهِ الَّذِى لَا إِلٰهَ إِلَّا هُوَ

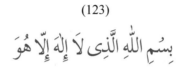

Bismillāhil lâdhī lā ilāhâ illā huwâ

In the name of Allāh. There is no deity save Him.

While getting dressed

(124)

اللّٰهُمَّ إِنِّى أَسْأَلُكَ مِنْ خَيْرِهِ وَخَيْرِ مَا هُوَ لَهُ، وَأَعُوذُ بِكَ
مِنْ شَرِّهِ وَشَرِّ مَا هُوَ لَهُ

Allāhûmmâ innī as'alûkâ khâyrihi wâkhayrî mā hûwâ lâhū. Wâ'a'oodhû bikâ min shârrîhi wa shârrî mā hûwâ lâhū

(122) Abu Dawūd, At-Tirmidhi, An-Nasā'i and Ibn Mājah

(123) Ibn-us-Sunni

O Allāh! I ask You the good in it and the good for which it is made and I seek Your protection from the evil in it and the evil for which it is made.

When mounting a means of transportation (car, train, plane etc.)

(125)

سُبْحَٰنَ ٱلَّذِى سَخَّرَ لَنَا هَٰذَا وَمَا كُنَّا لَهُۥ مُقْرِنِينَ
وَإِنَّآ إِلَىٰ رَبِّنَا لَمُنقَلِبُونَ

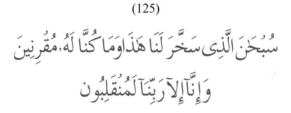

Subhānâl lâdhī sâkh-khârâ lânā hādhā wâmā kûnnā lâhū mûqrineen wâ'innā ilā râbbînā lâ mûnqâliboon

Glory to Him Who has subjected these for our (use), for we could never have accomplished this (by ourselves) and to our Lord surely we must turn back.

When retiring to sleep

(126)

بِاسْمِكَ رَبِّي وَضَعْتُ جَنْبِي وَبِكَ أَرْفَعُهُ ، إِنْ أَمْسَكْتَ
نَفْسِي فَاغْفِرْلَهَا ، وَإِنْ أَرْسَلْتَهَا فَاحْفَظْهَا بِمَا تَحْفَظُ بِهِ
عِبَادَكَ الصَّالِحِينَ

Bismikâ râbbī wâḍâ'tu jânbi wâbika ârfa'uhu in âmsâktâ nâfsī fâghfirlâhā wâ'in ârsâltâhā fâḥfâẓhā bimā tâḥfâẓu bihi 'ibādâkâs-ṣāliḥeen

---

(124) Ibn-us-Sunni

(125) Sūrâh Az-Zûkhrûf 43:13-14

(126) Al-Bukhāri, Muslim, Abu Dawūd, At-Tirmidhi, An-Nasā'i and Ibn Mājah

In Your name, O Lord, I lay my side (to sleep) and by (Your leave) I raise it up. So if You take away my soul (during sleep) forgive it and if You send it back (after sleep) protect it even as You protect Your pious servants.

Chapter Four:

Du‘ā’ for Special Occasions

I. In Personal Life

When looking in the mirror

(127)

اللَّهُمَّ أَنْتَ حَسَّنْتَ خَلْقِي فَحَسِّنْ خُلُقِي وَحَرِّمْ وَجْهِي
عَلَى النَّارِ، الْحَمْدُ لِلَّهِ الَّذِي سَوَّى خَلْقِي فَعَدَلَهُ، وَكَرَّمَ
صُورَةَ وَجْهِي فَأَحْسَنَهَا وَجَعَلَنِي مِنَ الْمُسْلِمِينَ

Allāhûmmâ ântâ ḥâssântâ khâlqī fâ hâssîn khûlûqī wâḥârrîm wâjhī 'alân-nār. Alḥâmdûlillāhil lâdhī sâwwā khâlqī fâ 'adâlâhu wâ kârrâmâ ṣoorâtâ wâjhī fâ aḥsânâhā. Wâja'alânī minâl muslimeen

O Allāh! You made my physical constitution good so make my disposition good too and keep my face safe from the hellfire. Grace be to Allāh Who fashioned and made me proportionate and honoured my face and made me of the Muslims.

In case of insomnia

(128)

اللَّهُمَّ رَبَّ السَّمٰوَاتِ السَّبْعِ وَمَا أَظَلَّتْ وَرَبَّ الْأَرَضِينَ وَمَا
أَقَلَّتْ وَرَبَّ الشَّيَاطِينِ وَمَا أَضَلَّتْ كُنْ لِي جَارًا مِنْ شَرِّ خَلْقِكَ
أَجْمَعِينَ أَنْ يَفْرُطَ عَلَيَّ أَحَدٌ مِنْهُمْ أَوْ أَنْ يَطْغَى، عَزَّ جَارُكَ، وَتَبَارَكَ اسْمُكَ

(127) Ibn Ḥibbān and Aṭ-Ṭâbârani

(128) Aṭ-Ṭâbârani

Allāhûmmâ râbbâs-sâmāwātîs-sab'î wâmā aẓâllât wârâbbâl ârâḍīnâ wâmā aqâllât wârâbbâsh-shayāṭīnâ wâmā aḍâllât kûn lī jārân min shârrî khâlqîkâ ajmâ'eena ay-yâfrûṭâ alayyâ âḥâdûm-minhûm aw ay-yâṭghā 'azzâ jārûkâ wâ tâbārâkâs-mûk

O Allāh! Lord of the seven firmaments and whatever they cover, Lord of the seven earths and whatever they contain, Creator of the devils and whoever they mislead, be my protector from the evil of all Your creatures lest some of them may hasten with insolence against me or trangress the bounds. Honoured is he who is in Your protection and blessed be Your name.

After a pleasant dream

(129)

اَلْحَمْدُ لِلّٰهِ الَّذِى بِنِعْمَتِهِ تَتِمُّ الصَّالِحَاتُ

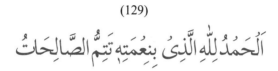

Alḥâmdûlillāhil lâdhī bî ni'mâtihī tâtîmmûṣ-ṣāliḥāt

Grace be to Allāh through Whose blessings good things are accomplished

After an unpleasant dream

(130)

اَلْحَمْدُ لِلّٰهِ عَلٰى كُلِّ حَالٍ

Alḥâmdûlillāhi 'alā kûllî ḥāl

Grace be to Allāh under all circumstances

(129) Al-Ḥakīm and Ibn Mājah

(130) Al-Ḥakīm and Ibn Mājah

On waking up after a nightmare

(131)

أَعُوذُ بِكَلِمَاتِ
اللَّهِ التَّامَّاتِ مِنْ غَضَبِهِ وَعِقَابِهِ وَشَرِّ عِبَادِهِ،
وَمِنْ هَمَزَاتِ الشَّيَاطِينِ وَأَنْ يَحْضُرُونِ

A'oodhû bikâlimātîl-
lāhittāmmātî mîn ghâḍâbîhī wâ 'iqābihī wâ shârrî 'ibādihī
wâmin hâmâzātish-shayāṭeen wâ'an yâḥḍûroon

I seek refuge in the perfect words of Allāh, from His displeasure and punishment and from evil people and from the (evil) promptings of devils and from their presence.

---

(131) Abu Dawūd, At-Tirmidhi and An-Nasā'i

II. On Social Occasions

When you see a Muslim brother smiling

(132)

أَضْحَكَ اللّٰهُ سِنَّكَ

Aḍḥâkâllāhu sînnâkâ

May Allah bring smiles to you

When told 'I love you'

(133)

أَحَبَّكَ الَّذِى أَحْبَبْتَنِى لَهُ

Aḥâbbâkâl-lâdhī aḥbâbtânī lâhū

May He, for Whose sake you love me, love you also

When a favour is done to you

(134)

جَزَاكَ اللّٰهُ خَيْرًا

Jâzākâllāhû khayrân

May Allāh give you a good reward

---

(132) Al-Bukhāri and Muslim

(133) Abu Dawūd, An-Nasā'i and Ibn Ḥibbān

(134) At-Tirmidhi

To someone who has got married

(135)

بَارَكَ اللّٰهُ لَكَ ، وَبَارَكَ عَلَيْكَ ، وَجَمَعَ بَيْنَكُمَا فِي خَيْرٍ

Bārâkâllāhû lâkâ wâbārâkâ 'alaykâ wâjâma'a baynâkûmā fī khayr

May Allāh bless (your spouse) for you and may He bless you and join you in a happy union.

At the beginning of intercourse

(136)

بِسْمِ اللّٰهِ ، اللَّهُمَّ جَنِّبْنَا الشَّيْطَانَ وَجَنِّبِ الشَّيْطَانَ مَا رَزَقْتَنَا

Bismillāhi allāhûmmâ jânnîbnâsh-shaytānâ wâ jânnîbish-shaytānâ mâ râzâqtânā

In the name of Allāh. O Allāh! Keep us away from satan and keep satan away from what You bestow on us (our children).

Prayer for small children

(137)

أُعِيذُكَ بِكَلِمَاتِ اللّٰهِ التَّامَّةِ ، مِنْ كُلِّ شَيْطَانٍ وَهَامَّةٍ وَمِنْ كُلِّ عَيْنٍ لَامَّةٍ

U'eedhûka bikâlimātîl-lāhittāmmâtî min kûllî shaytānin wahāmmâtin-wâ min kûllî 'aynîn lāmmâh

---

(135) Al-Bukhāri and Muslim

(136) Al-Bukhāri

(137) Al-Bukhāri

I seek refuge for you in the perfect words of Allāh, from every devil and every poisonous reptile and from every bad eye.

At the end of meetings or gatherings

(138)

سُبْحَانَكَ اللّٰهُمَّ وَبِحَمْدِكَ اَشْهَدُ اَنْ لَّا اِلٰهَ اِلَّا اَنْتَ
اَسْتَغْفِرُكَ وَاَتُوبُ اِلَيْكَ

Subḥānâkâllāhûmmâ wâ biḥâmdikâ ash-hâdû ânlā ilāha illā ântâ âstâghfirûkâ wâ âtoobû ilayk

Glory and praise be to You, O Allāh! I bear witness that there is no deity except You. I beg of You Your forgiveness and I repent to You.

---

(138) Abu Dawūd and Al-Ḥakīm

III. On the Occasion of Travel

What to say to someone who is leaving

(139)

أَسْتَوْدِعُ اللّٰهَ دِينَكَ

وَأَمَانَتَكَ ، وَخَوَاتِيمَ عَمَلِكَ ، وَأَقْرَأُ عَلَيْكَ السَّلَامَ

Astawdî'ûllāhâ dīnâkâ
wâ âmānâtâkâ wâ khâwāteemâ 'amâlikâ wâ'aqrâ'û 'alâykâs sâlām

Unto Allāh do I commend your deen (*Islām*), your trust (i.e. family, property etc.) and the conclusions of your deeds and I recite *salām* (peace) upon you.

(140)

زَوَّدَكَ اللّٰهُ التَّقْوَى ،

وَغَفَرَ ذَنْبَكَ ، وَيَسَّرَ لَكَ الْخَيْرَ حَيْثُمَا كُنْتَ

Zâwwâdâkâl lāhût-tâqwâ
wâghâfârâ dhânbâkâ wâ yâssârâ lâkâl khayrâ haythûmā kûnt

May Allāh provide you with *tâqwâ* (Allāh consciousness), forgive your sins and facilitate good for you wherever you may be.

---

(139) At-Tirmidhi and An-Nasā'i

(140) At-Tirmidhi and An-Nasā'i

When bidding farwell (by the traveller)

(141)

أَسْتَوْدِعُكَ اللَّهَ الَّذِى لَا تَضِيعُ وَدَائِعُهُ

Astawdî'ûkâllāhâl lâdhī lā taḍee'û wâ dā'î'ûh

I commend you unto Allāh Whose trusts are never lost.

When setting out on a journey

(142)

اللَّهُمَّ بِكَ أَصُولُ ، وَبِكَ أَجُولُ ، وَبِكَ أَسِيرُ . اللَّهُمَّ إِنِّى
أَسأَلُكَ فِى سَفَرِى هٰذَا الْبِرَّ وَالتَّقْوَى ، وَمِنَ الْعَمَلِ مَاتَرْضَى .
اللَّهُمَّ هَوِّنْ عَلَيْنَا سَفَرَنَا هٰذَا وَاطْوِ عَنَّا بُعْدَهُ . اللَّهُمَّ
أَنْتَ الصَّاحِبُ فِى السَّفَرِ وَالْخَلِيفَةُ فِى الْأَهْلِ . اللَّهُمَّ إِنِّى
أَعُوذُ بِكَ مِنْ وَعْثَاءِ السَّفَرِ ، وَكَآبَةِ الْمَنْظَرِ ، وَسُوءِ
الْمُنقَلَبِ فِى الْمَالِ وَالْأَهْلِ وَالْوَلَدِ

Allāhûmmâ bîkâ âṣoolû wâbîkâ âjoolû wâbîkâ âseer. Allāhûmmâ innī âs'alûkâ fī sâfârī hādhâl bîrrâ wâttâqwā wâ minâl 'amâli mā târḍā. Allāhûmmâ hâwwân 'alaynā sâfârânā hādhā wâṭwi 'annā bû'dâh. Allāhûmmâ ântâs-ṣaḥibû fîs-sâfârî wâlkhâleefâtû fîl ahl. Allāhûmmâ innī a'oodhû bîkâ mîn wa'thā'îs-sâfâr wâkâ'ābâtil mânẓâr wâsoo 'îl mûnqâlâbî fîl māli wâl âhli wâl wâlâd

---

(141) Aṭ-Ṭâbârani

(142) Aḥmad and Muslim

O Allāh! It is with Your help that I struggle, move and walk. O Allāh! I beg of You in this journey, virtue, piety and good deeds which are acceptable to You. O Allāh! Make our journey easy for us and shorten for us its distance. O Allāh! You are the companion in the journey and the guardian protector of the household. O Allāh! I seek refuge in You from the difficulties of this journey and from the disagreeable sights and from unpleasant return to (my) wealth, household and children.

Upon returning from a journey

(143)

آئِبُونَ تَائِبُونَ عَابِدُونَ لِرَبِّنَا حَامِدُونَ

Ā'iboonâ, tā'iboonâ, 'ābidoonâ lîrâbbinā ḥāmîdoon

We are returners, repentants, worshippers and thankful to our Lord.

---

(143) Aḥmad and Muslim

IV. In Distress

When faced by a hardship

(144)

اللَّهُمَّ لَا سَهْلَ إِلَّا مَا جَعَلْتَهُ سَهْلًا، وَأَنْتَ تَجْعَلُ الْحَزْنَ إِذَا شِئْتَ سَهْلًا

Allāhûmmâ lā sâhlâ illā mā ja'altâhū sâhlân wa'antâ tâj'alûl ḥâznâ idhā shi'tâ sâhlâ

O Allāh! There is nothing easy except what You make easy and You make the difficult easy if it be Your will.

When a hope or desire could not be fulfilled

(145)

قَدَّرَ اللهُ وَمَا شَاءَ فَعَلَ

Qâddârâl lāhû wâmā shā'â fâ'âl

Allāh had decided and whatever He willed He did.

(144) Ibn Ḥibbān

(145) An-Nasā'i

When feeling angry

(146)

أَعُوذُ بِاللَّهِ مِنَ الشَّيْطَٰنِ الرَّجِيمِ

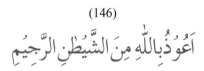

A'oodhû bîllāhî mînâsh-shaytān-nîr-râjeem

I seek refuge in Allāh from the accursed satan.

When overwhelmed by a problem

(147)

حَسْبُنَا اللَّهُ وَنِعْمَ الْوَكِيلُ

Ḥâsbûnâllāhu wâ nî'mâl wâkeel

Allāh suffices us and He is the best guardian.

When in pain (while placing one's hand over the location of the pain)

(148)

بِسْمِ اللَّهِ (ثَلَاثَ مَرَّاتٍ) ، أَعُوذُ بِعِزَّةِ اللَّهِ وَقُدْرَتِهِ مِنْ شَرِّ مَا
أَجِدُ وَأُحَاذِرُ (سَبْعَ مَرَّاتٍ)

Bîsmîllāh (3 times). *A'oodhû bî'izzâtîl-lāhî wâqûdrâtihī min sharrî mā âjidû wâ'uḥādhir* (7 times)

---

(146) Al-Bukhāri and Muslim

(147) Abu Dawūd

(148) Muslim

In the name of Allāh. I seek refuge in the Exalted Power and Glory of Allāh from that which I feel and fear.

When visiting a sick person (while patting the sick person)

(149)

اللّٰهُمَّ أَذْهِبَ الْبَاسَ رَبَّ النَّاسِ ، اِشْفِ وَأَنْتَ الشَّافِي ،
لَا شِفَاءَ إِلَّا شِفَاؤُكَ ، شِفَاءً لَا يُغَادِرُ سِقَماً

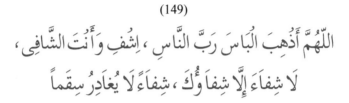

Allāhûmmâ adh-hîbâl bāsa râbbân nāsî îshfî wa'antash-shāfī
lā shîfā'a illā shîfā'ûkâ shîfā'a lā yughādirû sîqâmā

O Allāh! Remove the hardship, O Lord of mankind. Grant a cure for You are the healer. There is no cure but from You, a cure which leaves no illness behind.

At a time of disaster

(150)

إِنَّا لِلّٰهِ وَإِنَّا إِلَيْهِ رَاجِعُونَ ، اللّٰهُمَّ عِنْدَكَ أَحْتَسِبُ مُصِيبَتِي
فَأْجُرْنِي فِيهَا وَأَبْدِلْنِي مِنْهَا خَيْرًا

Innā lîllāhî wâ'innâ ilayhî rājî'oon. Allāhûmmâ 'indâkâ aḥtâsîbû muṣeebâtī
fa'jûrnī fīhā wâ'abdîlnī mînhā khayra

To Allāh we belong and to Him is our return. O Allāh! You suffice me in disaster, so reward me for it and replace it with something which is good.

---

(149) Al-Bukhāri

(150) At-Tirmidhi and Al-Ḥakīm

When offering condolences (to the family of the deceased)

(151)

إِنَّ لِلَّهِ مَاأَخَذَ وَلَهُ مَاأَعْطَى وَكُلُّ شَيْءٍ عِنْدَهُ
بِأَجَلٍ مُسَمًّى فَلْتَصْبِرْ وَلْتَحْتَسِبْ

Inna lîllāhî mā akhâdhâ wâlâhū mā a'tā wâkûllû shay'in 'indâhū bi'ajâlîm-mûsâmmā fâltâṣbîr waltâḥtâsib

Due is to Allāh that which He has taken away and His is whatever He has given. With Him, everything has an appointed term, so have patience and seek reward from Him.

When visiting the graveyard

(152)

السَّلَامُ عَلَيْكُمْ
أَهْلَ الدِّيَارِ مِنَ الْمُؤْمِنِينَ وَالْمُسْلِمِينَ ، وَيَرْحَمُ اللَّهُ
الْمُسْتَقْدِمِينَ مِنْكُمْ وَالْمُسْتَأْخِرِينَ ، وَإِنَّا إِنْ شَاءَ اللَّهُ بِكُمْ
لَاحِقُونَ ، أَسْأَلُ اللَّهَ لَنَا وَلَكُمُ الْعَافِيَةَ ، أَنْتُمْ لَنَا فَرَطٌ وَنَحْنُ
لَكُمْ تَبَعٌ ، اللَّهُمَّ لَا تَحْرِمْنَا أَجْرَهُمْ ، وَلَا تُضِلَّنَا بَعْدَهُمْ

Assâlāmû 'alâykûm
ahlâd-diyāri minâl mu'mîneenâ wâl muslimeenâ wâyârḥâmûl lāhûl mûstâqdîmeenâ minkûm wâl mustā'khîreenâ wâ'innā inshā'Allāhû bîkûm

---

(151) Al-Bukhāri

(152) Muslim, An-Nasā'i and Ibn Mājah

lāḥîqoon. As'ālûl lāhâ lânā wâlâkûmûl 'āfiyâh ântûm lânā fârāṭûn wânâhnû lâkûm tâbâ'ûn. Allāhûmmâ lā taḥrimnā âjrâhûm wâlā tuḍillânā ba'dâhûm

Peace be upon you dwellers of these abodes, believers and Muslims. May Allāh have mercy on those of you who were first (to die) and those who were last. We will, whenever Allāh wills, join you. I beg of Allāh salvation for us and for you. You preceded us and we will follow you. O Allāh! Deprive us not from reward (similar to theirs) and lead us not astray after they are gone.

V. Others

Prayer for fulfillment of a need (*Ṣalātul Ḥājah*)

Whoever is need of anything from Allāh ﷻ or from any son of Adam, then he should perform wuḍū' (ablution) in a nice way and then say two raka't of ṣalāh (prayer); he should then praise Allāh (*Alḥâmdûlillāhi râbbîl 'ālâmeen)* and send peace and blessings upon the Prophet ﷺ *Allāhûmmâ ṣâlli 'alā Muḥâmmâdîn*) then he should say:

(153)

لَا إِلٰهَ إِلَّا اللّٰهُ الْحَلِيمُ الْكَرِيمُ، سُبْحَانَ اللّٰهِ رَبِّ الْعَرْشِ الْعَظِيمِ، الْحَمْدُ لِلّٰهِ رَبِّ الْعَالَمِينَ، أَسْأَلُكَ مُوجِبَاتِ رَحْمَتِكَ وَعَزَائِمَ مَغْفِرَتِكَ، وَالْعِصْمَةَ مِنْ كُلِّ ذَنْبٍ، وَالْغَنِيمَةَ مِنْ كُلِّ بِرٍّ، وَالسَّلَامَةَ مِنْ كُلِّ إِثْمٍ، لَا تَدَعْ لِي ذَنْبًا إِلَّا غَفَرْتَهُ، وَلَا هَمًّا إِلَّا فَرَّجْتَهُ، وَلَا حَاجَةً هِيَ لَكَ رِضًا إِلَّا قَضَيْتَهَا يَا أَرْحَمَ الرَّاحِمِينَ

Lā ilāhâ illâllāhûl ḥâleemûl kâreem. Sûbhānâl lāhi râbbîl 'arshîl 'aẓeem. Alḥâmdûlillāhi râbbîl 'ālâmeen; as'alûkâ mujîbātî râḥmâtikâ wâ 'azā'ima mâghfirâtîkâ wâl 'iṣmâtâ mîn kûlli dhânbîn wâlghâneemâtâ min kûllî bîrrîn wâssâlāmâtâ min kûllî ithm. Lā tâda'lī dhâmbân illā ghâfârtâh; wâlā hâmmân illā fârrâjtâh; wâlā hājâtân hīya lâkâ riḍan illā qâḍaytâhā yā arḥâmâr-rāḥîmeen

There is no deity but Allāh, Most Forebearing, Supreme in honour. Glory be to Allāh, Lord of the Great Throne. Praise be to Allāh, Lord of the universe. O Allāh! I seek of You the means of (deserving) Your mercy, the means of (ascertaining) Your forgiveness, the protection from all mistakes, the benefit from all virtue and the freedom from all sins. O Allāh! Leave no mistake of mine without Your forgiveness, nor any stress without Your relief, nor any

(153) At-Tirmidhi, An-Nasā'i and Ibn Mājah

need of which You approve without being fulfilled by You,
O Most Merciful of the merciful.

(After reciting this du‘ā’, one should state the specific need for which the du‘ā’ was made. It may be for this world or the Hereafter. And it is He Who disposes, decrees and apportions.)

When seeking guidance in decision-making (*Istikhārah*)

(154)

اللَّهُمَّ إِنِّي أَسْتَخِيرُكَ بِعِلْمِكَ ، وَأَسْتَقْدِرُكَ بِقُدْرَتِكَ ، وَأَسْأَلُكَ
مِنْ فَضْلِكَ الْعَظِيمِ ، فَإِنَّكَ تَقْدِرُ وَلَا أَقْدِرُ ، وَتَعْلَمُ وَلَا أَعْلَمُ ، وَأَنْتَ
عَلَّامُ الْغُيُوبِ . اللَّهُمَّ إِنْ كُنْتَ تَعْلَمُ أَنَّ هَذَا الْأَمْرَ خَيْرٌ لِي فِي
دِينِي وَمَعَاشِي وَعَاقِبَةِ أَمْرِي - أَوْ قَالَ عَاجِلِ أَمْرِي وَآجِلِهِ -
فَاقْدُرْهُ لِي وَيَسِّرْهُ لِي ثُمَّ بَارِكْ لِي فِيهِ ، وَإِنْ كُنْتَ تَعْلَمُ
أَنَّ هَذَا الْأَمْرَ شَرٌّ لِي فِي دِينِي وَمَعَاشِي وَعَاقِبَةِ أَمْرِي -
أَوْ قَالَ فِي عَاجِلِ أَمْرِي وَآجِلِهِ - فَاصْرِفْهُ عَنِّي ، وَاصْرِفْنِي
عَنْهُ ، وَاقْدُرْ لِي الْخَيْرَ حَيْثُ كَانَ ثُمَّ ارْضِنِي بِهِ

Allāhûmmâ innī âstâkheerûkâ bî‘ilmîkâ wâ’âstâqdîrûkâ bîqûdrâtîkâ wâ’âs’alûkâ min fâḍlikâl ‘ạzeemî fâ’innâkâ tâqdirû wâlā âqdîrû wâta‘lamû wâlā a‘lâmû wâ’antâ ‘allāmûl ghuyoob. Allāhûmmâ in kûntâ ta‘lamû anna (hādhal amrâ) khayrûl-lī fi deenī wâma‘ashī wâ ‘āqibâti amrī - au qāla ‘ājîlî amrī wâ’ājilîhi - fâqdûrhû lī wâyâssîrhû lī thûmmâ bārîk lī fihî wâ’in kûntâ ta‘lamû anna (hādhal amra) sharrûl lī fi deenī wâma‘ashī wâ ‘āqibâti amrī - au qāla fi ‘ājîlî amrī wâ’ājilîhi – fâsrîfhû ‘annee wâsrîfnee ânhû wâqdûr līyal khayrâ haythû kānâ thûmmâ arḍinī bîh.

---

(154) Al-Bukhāri

O Allāh! I seek Your guidance (in making a choice) by virtue of Your knowledge and I seek ability by virtue of Your power and I ask You of Your great bounty. You have power and I have none and You know, I know not. You are the knower of hidden things. O Allāh! If in Your knowledge (this matter) is good for my religion, my livelihood and my affairs, immediate and distant, then ordain it for me, make it easy for me and bless it for me. And if in Your knowledge (this matter) is bad for my religion, my livelihood and my affairs, immediate and distant, then turn it away from me and turn me away from it and ordain for me the good wherever it may be and make me pleased with it.

Notes:

1. The above du'ā' is to be recited when there is uncertainty about the advisability of taking a decision, provided that it is Islamically permissible.
2. After performing wuḍū, one should offer two rak'āt of ṣalāh (sûnnah required for this purpose)
3. Before reciting the du'ā' it should be ascertained that the person is not already inclined to a given decision; otherwise it means that the person is not serious about seeking the guidance of Allāh.
4. In making this du'ā', the actual matter or decision concerning which Divine Guidance is being sought should be mentioned instead of the words (*hādhal amra*) (this matter).
5. After reciting the du'ā' (immediately or later on), one may feel more favourably disposed towards one choice or the other.

When one wakes up for night prayers (*Tâhâjjûd*)

(155)

اللَّهُمَّ لَكَ الحَمْدُ أَنتَ قَيِّمُ السَّمَوَاتِ وَالأَرْضِ وَمَنْ فِيهِنَّ ، وَلَكَ الحَمْدُ لَكَ مُلْكُ السَّمَوَاتِ وَالأَرْضِ وَمَنْ فِيهِنَّ ، وَلَكَ الحَمْدُ أَنتَ نُورُ السَّمَوَاتِ وَالأَرْضِ وَمَنْ فِيهِنَّ ، وَلَكَ الحَمْدُ أَنتَ الحَقُّ ، وَوَعْدُكَ الحَقُّ ، وَلِقَاؤُكَ حَقٌّ ، وَقَوْلُكَ حَقٌّ ، وَالجَنَّةُ حَقٌّ وَالنَّارُ حَقٌّ ، وَالنَّبِيُّونَ حَقٌّ ، وَمُحَمَّدٌ صلى اللّٰهُ عليهِ وَسلم حَقٌّ ، وَالسَّاعَةُ حَقٌّ ، اللَّهُمَّ لَكَ أَسْلَمْتُ ، وَبِكَ آمَنْتُ ، وَعَلَيْكَ تَوَكَّلْتُ ، وَإِلَيْكَ أَنَبْتُ ، وَبِكَ خَاصَمْتُ ، وَإِلَيْكَ حَاكَمْتُ ، فَاغْفِرْ لِي مَا قَدَّمْتُ وَمَا أَخَّرْتُ ، وَمَا أَسْرَرْتُ وَمَا أَعْلَنْتُ ، وَمَا أَنتَ أَعْلَمُ بِهِ مِنِّي ، أَنتَ المُقَدِّمُ وَأَنتَ المُؤَخِّرُ ، لَا إِلَٰهَ إِلَّا أَنتَ ، وَلَا حَوْلَ وَلَا قُوَّةَ إِلَّا بِاللهِ

Allāhûmmâ lâkâl ḥamdû ântâ qayyîmûs-samāwātî wâl arḍî wâmân fīhînnâ wâlâkâl ḥamdû lâkâ mûlkûs-samāwātî wâl arḍî wâmân fīhînnâ wâlâkâl ḥamdû ântâ noorûs- samāwātî wâl arḍî wâmân fīhînnâ wâlâkâl ḥamdû ântâl ḥaqqû wâwa'dûkâl ḥaqqû wâlîqā'ûka ḥaqqû wâqaulûka ḥaqqû wâljânnâtû ḥaqqû wânnārû ḥaqqû wânnâbiyyūnâ ḥaqqû wâmuḥâmmâdû ṣâllâllāhû alayhi wâsâllâmâ ḥaqqû wassa'atû ḥaqq. Allāhûmmâ lâkâ âslâmtû wabîkâ āmantû wâ 'alaykâ tâwâkkâltû wâ ilaykâ anâbtû wabîkâ khāṣamtû wâ ilaykâ ḥākâmtû fâghfirlī mā qâddâmmtû wâmā âkh-khârtû wâmā âsrârtû wâmā a'lântû wâmā ântâ a'lamû bîhī mînnī ântâl mûqâddîmû wâ ântâl mu'akh-khirâ lā ilāhâ illā ântâ wâlā hawlâ wâlā qūwwâtâ illā bîllāh

---

(155) Al-Bukhāri

All praise is due to You, O Allāh! You are the Sustainer of the heavens and the earth and whatever is in them. Praise be to You; Yours is the domain of the heavens and the earth and whatever is in them. Praise be to You; You are the light of the heavens and the earth and whatever is in them. Praise be to you. You are the Truth. Your promise is true, meeting with You is true. Your word is true, Paradise is true, Hell is true, Prophets are true, Muḥâmmâd ﷺ is true, the Hour (of Judgement) is true. O Allāh! Unto You do I submit, in You do I believe , upon You do I depend, unto You do I turn, for you do I contend, unto You do I seek judgement. So forgive me for what I have done and will do, for what I concealed and what I declared and for that of which You are more knowledgeable than me. You are the expediter and You are the Deferrer. There is no deity but You and there is no ability or power except by the leave of Allāh.